# DATA

# DATA

SETH ABRAMSON

BLAZEVOX[BOOKS]
*Buffalo, New York*

DATA
by Seth Abramson
Copyright © 2016

Published by BlazeVOX [books]



Printed in the United States of America

Interior design and typesetting by Geoffrey Gatza
Cover Art by Seamus Moran

First Edition
ISBN: 978-1-60964-246-4
Library of Congress Control Number: 2016930931

BlazeVOX [books]
131 Euclid Ave
Kenmore, NY 14217

Editor@blazevox.org

publisher of weird little books

# BlazeVOX [ books ]

blazevox.org

21 20 19 18 17 16 15 14 13 12 01 02 03 04 05 06 07 08 09 10

BlazeVOX

# Table of Contents

# DATA

*DATA* comprises original, appropriated, and remixed material. Each work is the result of a conceptual constraint; brief descriptions of some of these constraints can be found at the back of the collection.

I

## WHITE PRIVILEGE

I crossed a continent. I fell in love with a woman I'd never met. I lay in the fetal position as a woman I loved beat me. I masturbated in a synagogue. I ate kangaroo meat. I filled the bottom of a tent with vomit. I passed a kidney stone. I cried from constipation. I rowed across the Grand Canal at Versailles. I rode horses. I threatened my mother with a bat. I called a basketball game at the Palestra. My arches fell. I tobogganed down the Great Wall of China. I ate duck brains. *Rolling Stone* wrote about me twice. I slept with a married woman. I was in a Billy Joel cover band. I went to an anime convention in Copenhagen. I spent Wednesday afternoons with a six year-old whose fingers had been shot off. I littered in the Forbidden City. I won a first-degree murder trial. I have an irregular heartbeat. I'm a two-finger typist. I type 75 words per minute. I ate snails in a Paris alley. I was a stepfather-to-be. I had phone sex with the chief spokeswoman for Halliburton. I played on thirty-two athletic teams. I sang in a doo wop group. I held a dog as she died. I lost half a tooth in a biking accident. I totaled my car. I traveled to within an hour of the North Pole. My cholesterol is 204. I walked through human feces. I was a National Merit Scholar. I drove famous authors to airports and restaurants. I saw the Northern Lights over Sweden. My feces is green. I bought my abuser a necklace in Old San Juan. I'm a class D driver. My shirt size is 17½/32-33. My Klout score is 59. I was a best man. I married my sister. I went on a first date in a cemetery. I watched *Guiding Light* every day. I had an ileus. I received an anal probe while high in an ER. I'm from Massachusetts. I'm in Norway. I'm a godfather. I have an innie. A chicken quill punctured my uvula. I testified in federal court. In the dark I go blind in one eye. I have neuropathy in my right arm. I waited for a friend in a Canadian brothel. I went on a road trip with a former Tampa Bay Buccaneer. I was assaulted in a junkyard in Virginia. I'm a youngest child. I have a strong sense of smell. I'm a light snorer. I was burglarized in New

Hampshire. I took a sleeper from Beijing to Xi'an. I turned down $150,000. I collected bottles of urine under my bed. I assaulted my sister. I faked being able to play tennis. I played in a basketball league for Jews. I'm a tennis instructor. I pee sitting down. I make $11,324 a year. My penis length is above average. I wrote a novel at age fourteen. I have a cowlick. I don't know my father's birthday. I marched with one of the nation's top university marching bands. I drank forty year-old wine. I brought a pig into my dorm room. I have German blood. I get regular styes. I suffer from blepharitis. My jean size is 36x28. I rushed the field at Camp Randall Stadium. I share a publisher with J.K. Rowling. I saw ballgames in ten MLB ballparks. I'm ticklish. I lectured on post-postmodernism to architects at University of Michigan. I blurbed books by fellow poets. I reported on Division I college football. I was talked about in *Playboy*. I tore a bicep. I have only two memories from before the age of eight. I bird-watched. I wrote an article 20,000 people shared and 130,000 "liked" on Facebook. I'm an Assistant Professor of English. I named the university program, department, and college I work in. I have an Internet addiction. I bleed daily from my bellybutton. I subtweeted. I watched a homicide trial at the Old Bailey. I wrote an essay that was translated into six languages. I declined an interview with a Turkish television station. I shat myself three times. I trimmed my habitually unruly pubes. I was the victim of a road rage assault. I visited a micro-nation. I was interviewed by *The New York Times*. A newspaper photographer took pictures of my living room wall. I spent a summer making alphabetized lists of pistols, rifles, shotguns, submachine guns, machine guns, sports cars, tanks, fighter jets, survival gear, and knives. I was seconds from killing myself. I rolled pennies to buy lunch. I convinced a child to sell me his video games. I saved the life of someone I loved. I lusted after a stripper. My blood pressure is 129/87. I comforted my fiancée during a seizure. I wrote fifteen hundred poems. I achieved advanced proficiency in French. I was the first blogger listed on Google News. I couldn't make rent. I broke a national political scandal in the media. I said "I love you" twenty times in a row. I called 911 six times. I filmed an unreleased music video. I spent $6,000 on Legos. I twice lost thirty pounds in thirty days. I walked out on my MFA graduation. My nose is crooked. I saw a hundred Van Goghs on weed. I rode in an ambulance. I saw ten firework displays in under two hours. I gave away a cat I loved. I learned to vaporize in the home of a famous novelist. I ran a corporation for three years. I've had plastic surgery. For two years I slept in a bed where someone had twice attempted suicide. I'm Generation X. I got a 1360 on the SAT. I don't know my blood type. I was chased by my father. I climbed a hill in Alabama. I was ordered to wear a rubber glove in the water. I stood on a hill above the Barents Sea. I rescued hundreds from wrongful imprisonment. My eyesight varies from day to day. I threatened a police officer. A judge told me to shut up. I have Russian blood. A Supreme Court Justice compared my motions practice to a blunderbuss. My resting heart rate is 73. A woman told me she saw an angel on my shoulder. A friend tried to flush herself down a toilet. I've never lived in a detached building. I smoked cigars at a camp for children. I threw up on an ER doctor. I watched the sun set from the steps of Sacre Coeur. I biked through rural villages in China. I saw my father's penis. I threw up on an EMT. I drove under the influence. I cried at two hundred movies. I lost my virginity before I'd kissed a girl. I'm a webmaster. My first love was a black girl from Dallas. I stood atop the Article Circle. I asked a model to marry me and she said yes. I applied to Oxford for love of a woman. I applied to the Iowa Writers' Workshop for love of a woman. I had a radio talk show. I paid for someone else's cocaine. I was the last student admitted to Dartmouth College in 1994. I'm bad with directions. A murderer threatened to kill me. A fourteen year-old heroin addict wanted to date me. I threw the New Hampshire Attorney General out of a room. I threw a U.S. Senator out of a room. I awoke with ants in my hair three days running. I lost my virginity at nineteen. I have Polish blood. I took a slow boat to China. I rafted down a waterfall. I didn't use a condom until I was twenty-six. I had sex while watching pornography with a prize-winning British poet. My best friend spent a week watching TV with Jodie Foster. I watched a man beat his child. My best friend became an Alaskan folk singer. I was questioned by police officers in my living room in New Hampshire. I studied Con Law with Ronald Reagan's Solicitor General. I studied Urban Ed with a member of the Nixon and Ford Administrations. My penis girth is above average. I was questioned by police officers in my living room in Wisconsin. My best friend was a wide receiver for the University of Texas. I was diagnosed with low-grade PTSD. I've had one cavity. I'm not a morning person. I wore a heart monitor while lecturing to undergraduates. I wrote an essay for *The Washington Post* on the abolition of the creative writing workshop. I'm a bad driver. I was fired for being incompetent with a meat slicer. I started to drink too much. I don't believe anything matters. I can make myself urinate by singing "Waterfalls" by TLC. I worked my first homicide at age twenty-three. A man told me I had the protection of the Hell's Angels. I refused an illegal payment in an elevator. A man sent me a Christmas card after threatening to kill me. I was the only white person for miles. I tutored scientists. I kissed a woman in the Louvre. I pulled a muscle in Vancouver. I have a Chinese visa. I saw FLOTUS at the Summer Palace. John Darnielle sweated on me. I'm backstage with Animal Collective. I inspired a country album. I hugged a woman for eighteen minutes. I was embroiled in an international scandal. *Pitchfork* wrote about me. I'm a Kohen. I hung out with crustpunks at the corner of Haight and Ashbury. I ran through a cornfield. I drove through a riot in Boston. I saw The National open for Barack Obama. A country singer called out my name during a concert. I was hounded by reporters. I was 1,000 feet from a tornado. I was discussed on white nationalist websites. An anti-Semitic cyber-terrorist demanded my death. I deliberately urinated on my roommate's bedding. My best friend argued cases before the New Hampshire Supreme Court. I wrote a bestselling book. My best friend runs 4% of Chicago's elementary schools. A novelist with Simon & Schuster called me the best parallel parker she'd ever seen. My best friend is twelve years younger than me. I told a London prostitute we couldn't fuck because I was on vacation. I often forget my age. I cross-examined patrolmen. I represented rape victims. A man published literary snuff porn about me. I held a service pistol. I collapsed on a staircase. I said "I love you" over a thousand times. A novelist wrote a short story about me. My favorite poet snorted cocaine off a bathtub, then said he'd been dying to meet me. I won three national poetry prizes. The Editor of *Poetry* unfriended and unfollowed me. A Pulitzer Prize winner sent me abusive emails. I refused a bribe from the Boston Red Sox. Someone I loved vandalized my property. I was a political commentator for Air America Radio. I get skin tags. I have a gag reflex. My IQ is 137. My BMI is 34.83. I gave readings and lectures in fifteen states. I stood on the field at Fenway Park. I got a rimjob. I drove to Pittsburgh on a whim. I spoke to my girlfriend on the phone for fourteen hours. I translated for Spanish speakers in criminal cases. I tutored children in Hebrew. I got fleas. I babysat. I talked men out of suicide. I was stalked and slandered. I told the Hillsborough County Attorney I was off my meds. I wore women's underwear. I suffer from clinical depression. I sweat when it's over seventy. I've sweated in temperatures below zero. I barely spoke to my sister for years. A woman told me I'd been born to the perfect American family. A man told me I'd been sent to him by Jesus Christ. A prosecutor tried to convert me to Christianity in a conference room. I failed three dozen swim tests. I canoed with my father. I threw a birthday party at a museum. I met a friend of Clarence Darrow. I swore an oath to never masturbate again. I memorized dialogue from ten animated films. An object moving at fifty miles per hour hit me in the face. I fractured a finger. I broke promises. I launched a literary magazine. I read a 2,700-page epic three times. I met Maurice Sendak. An ex wrote a song about me. An ex wrote a poem about me. An ex wrote a chapbook about me. An ex wrote a full-length poetry collection about me. A stranger wrote a full-length poetry collection about me. I played a video game while men in Hazmat suits scoured the room for bacteria. I wrote 365 poems in a year. I loved a woman with wings on her back. I signed autographs. I lectured at the University of Amsterdam. I won an award for my fiction. I won honors for my teaching. My neighbor tried to buy cocaine from me. I was thrown off a golf course. A Stegner Fellow compared me to Hitler. A Stegner Fellow handed me the blade he cuts himself with. I laid in the fetal position on an ER floor. My best friend ended our friendship to spend more time with my ex. I detailed my kinks to a middle-aged woman. I have Lithuanian blood. I tore my groin stealing second. I won an award for my Spanish. My best friend ended our friendship because he didn't like how I looked when I ate. I spoke with firefighters outside my bedroom door. The House Minority Leader wanted me on a weekly conference call. I was mauled by a miniature schnauzer. I got a handjob in Walden Pond. I had sex at a museum. I had sex in a parking garage. I ejaculated and saw a shooting star simultaneously. I'm afraid of *The Muppet Show*. I cheated on a math test. I'm a Scorpio. I'm a fornicator. I was the fastest boy in my class. My HDL is 36. I can't add any more friends on Facebook. I was born on Halloween. I thought I was asexual until I was 19. I only root for underdogs. My debt-to-income ratio is ten to one. I had sex in a moving vehicle. I asked a therapist if I was a sociopath. I'm an uncle to four children. My mother asked if I wanted to switch schools. I trespassed. I drove recklessly. I'm a pariah. I vandalized. For nine months I couldn't maintain an erection. I suffer from automatonophobia. I suffer from megalophobia. A university hired security for my Q&A. I studied cartooning with Lynda Barry. I studied criminal law with Alan Dershowitz. I touched a dog inappropriately. I believed I suffered from "morning sickness" until I was sixteen. I masturbated at a friend's house. I wore a $60 anti-pollution mask. I ate hot dogs with a judge in a courthouse basement. I starred in a commercial. I wet my pants in a Kmart. I won trophies. 24,000 people visited my website in twenty-four hours. I slept with women within hours of meeting them. I sat in a dark stairwell with twelve black men in chains. Shia LaBeouf and Nick Searcy blocked me on Twitter. A man in London searches the Internet for my name every day. I'm light-sensitive. A delivery man said I was his favorite DJ. I was stopped by two different police departments in ten minutes. I was in a car chase. I wrote fifty-five pages of literary analysis in six hours. I marched with Communists in England. I set off metal detectors in government buildings repeatedly without consequence. The Chief Justice of the U.S. Supreme Court accused me of being a phony. My wedding band is the only jewelry I've ever worn. I embarrassed myself at a dinner with Monica Lewinsky's attorney. I proposed to a woman while standing in the Seine. I picked out baby names with my wife. I received a dozen suspicious-looking packages from China. I was born in the Cradle of America. I drove a motorboat in the Atlantic. I get post-nasal drip for months on end. I drove along the Pacific shore. I was a recluse for four years. I took five pills a day. I pissed on a fjord in Norway. I benefit from white privilege. I've seen my looks repulse women. I got married in a judge's office. I was last at a normative weight at age six. I threw out my back twice. I've supported a family other than my own. I lived with a man for eight months without speaking to him. They say I used to look like Tom Cruise. They say I used to look like Emilio Estevez. I've sold an engagement ring. I'm a notary public. I scored 1490 on the GRE. I'm a Justice of the Peace. My ring finger is longer than my index finger. I'm an officer of the court. I participated in twenty illicit midnight rendezvous. I spit into the wind on a Scottish beach. I searched a dead man's effects in an FBI field office. I have Romanian blood. I shattered a man's windshield with a rock. I almost died on a highway near Saskatoon. I got high at a professional conference. I saw *Frozen 3D* while high. I was cited by Romanian academics. I'm a columnist for a Scandinavian academic journal. I ejaculated into specimen containers. I almost drowned in a pool in South Carolina. I dream of disappearing. I protected a child from incest. My best friend was a pathological liar. My first crush moved to Australia the day after she told me she liked me. I judged the National Mock Trial Championships. I have a 4.0 GPA. Two policemen comforted me. I hid in my closet. I drove across the Golden Gate Bridge. I drove across the Lion's Gate Bridge. I spoke to a hundred men through holes in cell doors. I haggled with merchants in the Muslim Quarter of Xi'an. I ran through the rain to comfort a black woman whose dog had died. I drove for sixteen hours straight. I was told someone I cared for had hung himself. I worked for tips. I did thousands of hours of pro bono work. I fell into a pool at an art gallery. I received oral sex at truck stops. A blue jay and a cardinal were two of my best friends. I spoke off the record with powerful political operatives. I didn't lose a trial for eighteen months. I wrote for America's oldest college newspaper. I photographed crime scenes. I took statements from crime victims. A petition opposing my doctoral research went viral. I was lied to by police officers. I assisted in a courthouse escape. I edit an annual anthology of experimental writing. I got lost in the wilderness. I introduced Shia LaBeouf to metamodernism. I saved a marriage. I had sex under a Christmas tree. I had sex while looking in the mirror. I was broken up with on an empty beach. I was lied to about royalties. I lived in a room with no door for months. I was interviewed by Brazilian media. I took hammered dulcimer lessons. I took singing lessons. I took piano lessons. I took tennis lessons. I took swimming lessons. I got an A+ in Criminal Law. I got an A+ in Shakespeare. My best friend moved to Korea and I never saw him again. I stayed in hostels in Asia. I greened out. My best friend moved to California and I never saw him again. Jeremy Irons made a movie about my professor. I was on the cover of the nation's foremost poetry magazine. I was blacklisted by the nation's foremost poetry anthology. I resigned myself to dying in the next sixty seconds. I told someone I'd assault them if I ever saw them. Two people said they would assault me if they ever saw me. I met my wife on Twitter.

I'm agnostic. I'm a pescatarian. I'm as far north as you can go in Europe. I slept in the fetal position for ten years. I have GERD. I have cup ears. I have a severe vitamin D deficiency. I'm a baritone. I've never voted Republican. I threw out a Christmas tree at 2AM on May 18th. My best friend was a multimillionaire. My best friend was a carpenter who lived in a log cabin. Jewish jokes were told in my presence. I received a cease-and-desist letter from Shia LaBeouf. I first scrambled an egg at thirty. I'm a tenure-track employee. The police called me Mr. Freeze. I chatted with a Norwegian pop star. My eyelashes are unusually long. My eyebrows are unusually long. My nose hair is unusually long. I walked fifty-five miles in six days. I published reviews of books I hadn't finished. I'm an arachnophobe. I own 33 *Dungeons & Dragons* guidebooks. My father likes attorney jokes. As a child I wanted to be an architect. I'd quit poetry if I could play the guitar. A bookstore clerk said I was famous. As a child I wanted to be Ivan Lendl. I spit in the Thames. I spit off the Great Wall. I smuggled undeclared goods across the Canadian border. I took back every woman who asked me to. I forgave every person who asked me for forgiveness. I took a cross-country flight that suffered a serious malfunction. I lost my singing voice in my twenties. I'm a metamodernist. I swore an oath to uphold the Constitution. I feel incompetent. I believe I have a faulty heart. I've been blackmailed. I've been libeled. I'm terrified by the N-word. I dislike atheism. I believe I'll die young. The head of my union tried to get me fired. I moved back home six years after graduating from Harvard Law. I live in the tallest residential building in northern New England. I climbed the southern tower of Cathédrale Notre-Dame de Paris. I ate fried chicken in a strip club. I'm in the capital of Texas. I'm in the largest city in Alaska. I have a hiatal hernia. I have a herniated disc. My two best friends thrust swastikas in my face. My first name and last name routinely get mispronounced and misspelled. I used electrical tape and nail polish to fix my car. I had homosexual daydreams. My name means Life. People call me Abe. I'm a bear. A friend of mine died of AIDS. Black classmates mocked my interracial relationship. I skipped 25% of my law school classes. My job gave me nightmares for years. I was called a "Jew lawyer" repeatedly. My publisher disavowed me. I saw Billy Joel at Wrigley. A domestic drone videotaped me in Union Park. I saw four blue-skinned men drumming. I swallowed semen. I was in a head-on collision. I went to Graceland 2. I was confronted by a carload of anti-Semites in Mississippi. I'm an expert on sixties psych-pop. I spoke on the phone for hours with a friend of Frank O'Hara. I grew up in a rural village. The state bar identified me as a future leader. A stripper performed in my living room. I didn't have a table to eat at for six years. Online tests say I'm Lawful and Good. I was unfriended and unfollowed by hundreds. I rushed to the aid of a stroke victim. I represented more than 2,000 defendants. I remixed the words of a mass murderer. I don't like being touched. I cry easily. My favorite number is 8. I admire my wife more than anyone I know. I started graying from stress. My shoe size is 9. My triglycerides are 187. My lips are chronically chapped. I've never had a professional conduct complaint. A video game made me cry. I permanently injured my nose. I've had cybersex forty times. People call me Jules. I own 62 baseball caps. I own more than 5,000 CDs. I biked the length of the second-oldest city wall in China. People call me Pablo. People call me Madrigal. People call me Chaim. People call me Stuey. I have a hairy back. There are people who'd like me dead. I suffer from vertigo. I have Steve Blass Disease. I'm an INFP. I was a halfback. I was a winger. I was a pitcher. I was a catcher. I only played catch with my father once. I drove the length of an eight-mile tunnel. I was offered a job by the Association of Writers and Writing Programs. I gave a reading in an anarchist bookstore. I was injected with typhoid. I sat in the well of the U.S. House of Representatives. A state university called me a "dream hire." I cough at least once a minute. My Gmail account was tagged as a spambot. I'm bad at social media. My elementary school was founded by hippies. My body hair disgusts people. I admire my parents. I insulted my teacher. I ran red lights. I asked the police to find my girlfriend before she killed herself. My roommate said his ideal woman would have the body of a prisoner in Auschwitz. I'm a supertaster. I'm a self-talker. I'm a Scandophile. Pennies were thrown at my feet. I itemized my faults once a week for five years. My eyes are the color of shit. I'm a color commentator. My favorite color is blue. I wish my eyes were blue. I'm between 5'8" and 5'9". I slow-danced with a woman in an empty movie theater. I masturbated wrong for years. I've been scared of myself. My hair loss is Class 5 on the Norwood Scale. I don't like being looked at. I've been mistaken for a homeless man. I've been mistaken for a rich man. I was handed an illegal inspection sticker for my car. I work at the University of New Hampshire. I lost my mojo. I like to be naked in the house. I drove with illegal plates for six years. I've gone without underwear. I haven't had a good night's sleep in years. I'm allergic to antibiotic eye ointments. I'm submissive in bed. I'm dominant in bed. I'm middling in bed. I shattered a glass bottle in a pharmacy. I taught grammar to electrical engineers and national guardsmen. I spent a year believing my bedmate would stab me. I've been rejected for admission by twelve schools. I think I have premature dementia. I'm not an Anglo. I'm an Anglophile. My wife calls me Hubs. I didn't have a gay friend until college. I didn't have a lesbian friend until I was 34. I was hounded by reporters. I'm a Dungeon Master. I made my first black friend at age six. I'm a tenth-level Ranger. I was subpoenaed. I've lied about my name, age, and gender. I'm a criminal. I have birthmarks on my chest. I have a permanent scar on my forehead. I won an award for being good with children. I was a two-time Little League All-Star. I was Vice President of a choir. I charge $30/hour for copy-editing. I was paid $22/hour as an attorney. I'm exhausted. I'm better with faces than names.

## STRANGERS

Seth Abramson, your days of abuse and self-revision are over. In case you forgot, Seth Abramson is a scumbag who tries to profit from and threaten poets with his Harvard lawyering. We're watching Seth Abramson's public implosion with a mix of pity and *what the fuck*. Seth Abramson's attempts to shame and silence others by calling them crazy tell you everything you need to know about his other thoughts. I swear to God, we all just have to ignore Seth Abramson. It's what Seth Abramson does: freak out online and then erase the evidence. Seth Abramson is like Walter White and Stuart Smalley joining forces to save poetry from poets. I wonder if Seth Abramson makes love as delicately as he tweets? Hell, at this point you might as well unfollow Seth Abramson. Seth Abramson uses the mass murder of women to promote his sick poetry. Seth Abramson is jealous he can't rock a beard and his opinions mean nothing: #fuckyou. Seth Abramson is bullshit. Seth Abramson is a vile poetry troll who has hit a new rock bottom. Montana is awesome, Seth Abramson is not. Why is Seth Abramson a bitch? Let me count the ways. Only a little bitch would have a picture of Keanu Reeves on his blog instead of himself. Only a little bitch would wear this scarf. Seth wants to be one of the cool kids, so he sucks up to the avant-garde. The reason Seth Abramson does not allow anonymous comments is because he's not actually interested in the truth from strangers. Seth Abramson is utterly delusional and has no clue what he's talking about. Seth Abramson and his ongoing lack of professionalism are pathetic. I dreamt Seth Abramson was breaking walnuts with his superhero erection, and awoke to my wife tapping my forehead with an ordinary spoon. Seth Abramson has an irrational and completely unprofessional savior complex. Seth Abramson needs a trip to the Jackie Derrida Memorial Rehab Clinic. No, I *don't* want to follow Seth Abramson. Seth Abramson is a bizarre hoax artist. Let Seth Abramson write his quasi-scientific, multi-dimensional, metaphysical literary babble. I completely forgot the name of that murderer kid from California—I think it was Seth Abramson? Seth Abramson has moved up to #3 in Poetry and #1 in Self-Promotion in my annual ranking of douchebaggery. Seth Abramson has a twisted modus operandi. Seth Abramson is vile and opportunistic and should be fired. Seth Abramson is capitalism at its worst. Even the *Wall Street Journal* is behaving better than Seth Abramson. Can we please, now, all of us at once, stop giving a shit about *anything* Seth Abramson says? Please? Seth Abramson is distasteful beyond all reason. Seth Abramson is fucking obnoxious. Dear everyone in the creative writing world: never *ever* take Seth Abramson seriously again. I have no respect for Seth Abramson at all. There's a reason I blocked Seth Abramson on Twitter. I was seething with viscous anger about Seth Abramson before it was cool. I bet a Seth Abramson sex tape would sell like wildfire. Seth Abramson is an angry virgin. Seth Abramson is boring. The next Olympics could be held inside Seth Abramson. We are dismayed, disheartened, and distressed by Seth Abramson. If I ever see Seth Abramson, I'm going to punch him in the face. Seth Abramson is the worst writer in America. Is it too late for Seth Abramson to write a really shitty and insensitive poem about Michael Brown? I'm asking for a friend. Seth Abramson is a back-scratcher. Seth Abramson is a humorless tight-ass. Seth Abramson is a loose cannon, not someone I'd want to ask for advice about anything. Only Robert Olen Butler is more passive-aggressive than Seth Abramson. Seth Abramson, your anus is an unforgivable plot hole. Seth Abramson is a vortex of bullshit. Seth Abramson is a little limp-dick fuck who gets excited at the keyboard. Seth Abramson is an asshole; I hope he drops dead in a pool of his own filthy spooge. Seth Abramson's got me so excited I'm typing with abandon, frothing at the fingertips for another one of his run-on sentences heavy with subclauses and those obnoxious parentheticals he throws in like so many peppercorns in a too-tossed salad. Seth Abramson is a stodgy fucking prick who used to get beat by his ex-girlfriend. Seth Abramson is the L. Ron Hubbard of poetry. Seth Abramson is a pompous blowhard. Seth Abramson has an ego that would make Kanye West embarrassed. Seth Abramson should have been spanked as a child. Seth Abramson is a snake-oil salesman. Seth Abramson is aggressively desperate and it's hilarious. Seth Abramson has no integrity. The verbose Seth Abramson would make a great politician. An article by Seth Abramson on MFA programs can only be and only is a long infomercial for Seth Abramson. It's okay to write rape porn about Seth Abramson because that guy begs for it. *Seth Abramson grabbed her. Threw her to the ground. Pulled off her pants. Ripped off her panties. Mounted her. Seth Abramson's young pink balls rubbed painfully against her hairy twat. O Lord, he thought. O Lord. O Lord. And finally Seth Abramson collapsed in a young boy's cumless climax. She pressed charges. Seth Abramson was arrested. But when they examined her they found no traces of semen or forced entry. And when they examined Seth Abramson it all made sense: he had a house-mouse cock.* I wonder if critics of Seth Abramson have gone too far? Is there some level of respect being passed over, involving Seth Abramson's sexual habits being played out publicly? I want to throw up all over Seth Abramson. Seth Abramson misrepresents himself. Seth Abramson is sketchy. Seth Abramson is tawdry and sad. Seth Abramson stopped all conversation and made it into a money thing. Seth Abramson said he wouldn't help anyone unless they paid him. Seth Abramson is a blatant self-promoter. Seth Abramson is a coward. Seth Abramson is a sniveling, insecure little weasel. Seth Abramson reminds me of a female circumcisionist, a warmonger, or a heroin salesman. Seth Abramson runs a racket. I really hope this ruins Seth Abramson's career. I guarantee Seth Abramson threatened to sue that guy. Seth Abramson is a lecherous blight. I'm disgusted by Seth Abramson. Seth Abramson is a shark. For Seth Abramson to call himself a poet as a way to conjure nobility and condone reckless pathology without action is cowardice. Seth Abramson will have no career. Seth Abramson targeted specific poets to call them *crazy, insane,* or *drug addicts.* I will publicly invoke a petition to remove Seth Abramson's book from his press's list if he doesn't apologize, not that any apology he made would be sincere. Our narrow community has somehow allowed Seth Abramson to invade it. Seth Abramson is a sewer-dweller. Seth Abramson should know we have poets in our community who follow through with their threats of assault. Seth Abramson shakes epithets around where his genitals should be. Seth Abramson should grow a pair. Seth Abramson makes people anxious, then profits from that anxiety. Seth Abramson is a soggy self-promotional shitstorm. Seth Abramson dupes people. Seth Abramson is reprehensible. Seth Abramson shuts people down and dismisses them if they have a contrary opinion. Seth Abramson is a crank. Seth Abramson is evil. Seth Abramson is pure greed. Seth Abramson is corrupt. Seth Abramson has donned a *kick me* sign. Seth Abramson's research methods are utterly bogus. Even a cursory glance at Seth Abramson's blog reveals how many extreme biases he has. Seth Abramson's work is partial, capricious, and undertaken by someone with no real qualifications. Seth Abramson's research is shabby and his results faulty. Seth Abramson's methods are ridiculously inadequate. Seth Abramson's comments are inappropriate and defamatory. Seth Abramson is a hijacker; he shouts down everyone else in the room. Seth Abramson has a bias against everyone who disagrees with him. Seth Abramson has a direct financial incentive for skewing his research. Seth Abramson's work is junk. Seth Abramson's research and writing are shoddy. Seth Abramson is obviously very dishonest. Seth Abramson's work is ridiculous. Every person I know who has ever interacted with Seth Abramson believes him to be dishonest. *Bend Seth Abramson under you, God. Face down, God. And make him bleed, God.* I've never seen anyone but Seth Abramson defend his work. Seth Abramson's work is borderline absurd. Wondering which is worse: the Broncos or Seth Abramson trying to sell his movement of one. Seth Abramson is the Bill O'Reilly of poetry. Seth Abramson is a sociopath. Seth

Abramson's work is silly and problematic. Seth Abramson's work is stupid. Seth Abramson's work is dangerous. Seth Abramson takes advantage of naive twenty-two year-olds. People insult Seth Abramson like it's going out of style. Seth Abramson has a propensity for making enemies, and making very attorneyesque arguments online simply tosses gas on the flames. Hatred of Seth Abramson is an amazing sideshow. There is a lot of Seth Abramson hatred out there. Seth Abramson has a massive reputation management problem. Seth Abramson is being publicly shamed. Seth Abramson is a scam artist. I think Seth Abramson's a little unsure of himself. Seth Abramson wrote about how we're all apparently idiots in *The Huffington Post*. Seth Abramson is tone-deaf and self-serving. The only thing unforgivable here is Seth Abramson's critical thinking. Seth Abramson is an idiot. Seth Abramson is lazy. Seth Abramson rubs me the wrong way. Seth Abramson is a literary horror. Seth Abramson gives off an aura of childishness and desperation. Seth Abramson is a blustering nerd, feverishly pushing his duct-taped glasses upward on his nose with his left forefinger. Seth Abramson offends me. Seth Abramson is a show-off. Writers, a group to which Seth Abramson doesn't belong, don't really care what a failed attorney in a sweater has to say to his webcam and are unaware of his existence. Seth Abramson is malicious. Seth Abramson is deceptive and malicious. Seth Abramson is a mismanager. Seth Abramson is quicksand. Seth Abramson is really sickening. Seth Abramson needs to go to the mall and buy something cashmere, maybe merino wool, because Seth Abramson is too old for a hoodie. Seth Abramson's blog is a pitiful piece of work. Seth Abramson is embarrassing. I just received a backchannel email reporting that Seth Abramson is finally getting laid. Seth Abramson feels authority and entitlement coursing through his veins. Seth Abramson is a lying, white, middle-aged U.S. conceptual poet. I looked deep into the heart of AWP and I saw sitting there, on a little chair, Seth Abramson. Seth Abramson is unethical. Seth Abramson's criticism is full of factual errors, assumptions, straw men, and backtracking. Seth Abramson's criticism is long-winded and bogged-down. Only real sadomasochists should click on Seth Abramson's links. I could rip Seth Abramson's criticism to shreds; it's glaringly false. I unfriended Seth Abramson because I was tired of seeing him bully people. *Seth Abramson choked on his own bile and died.* Seth Abramson's not worth my time. Seth Abramson is a fucking douchebag. Seth Abramson is obsessive. Seth Abramson is an ass. Seth Abramson is really rotten. Seth Abramson can't understand the idea that in the end he is a suck poet and a suck mind. Seth Abramson's research is an absurd blemish on otherwise fine work being done for this community. Seth Abramson is biased. I won't read any of Seth Abramson's responses unless a friend tells me I ought to. Seth Abramson is rude and unfair. Lots of people in the poetry world hate Seth Abramson. Seth Abramson takes a business-like approach to poetry. Seth Abramson behaves like a lawyer amidst a gaggle of poets. Seth Abramson is all about poetry as a growth market. Seth Abramson is a whiner. Seth Abramson is a bit childish. Seth Abramson likes to rant. Seth Abramson is short-sighted and has a narrow sensibility. Seth Abramson attacks other poets. Seth Abramson has astonishing verbal diarrhea. Posterity won't even say, "Seth Abramson who?" Seth Abramson isn't worthy of licking the shit off Derek Walcott's shoes. I've never seen such an absence of humility as I see in Seth Abramson. I've seen Seth Abramson's poetry, and he should give up. I've never encountered, outside mental health clinics or hospitals, a delusional personality to match Seth Abramson's. There is not the slightest trace of genuine fire in anything Seth Abramson writes. Seth Abramson has absolutely no hope of even *emulating* real artists. In the future Seth Abramson will not even rate a footnote. It's going to take me all of a half hour to forget Seth Abramson. Seth Abramson is a puritanical, self-righteous little cocksucker. Seth Abramson is mean-spirited and envious. Seth Abramson is disrespectful beyond belief. Seth Abramson refuses to have an inner life. Seth Abramson hides behind a wall of anonymity. Seth Abramson is contemptible. Until Seth Abramson becomes a public figure, he will never understand the collective hurt blogs cause. Seth Abramson's psychology is spooky. Seth Abramson is a finely trained entity who capably resists introspection. Seth Abramson participates in evil. Seth Abramson's skull is made of lead. Seth Abramson does not know who the fuck he is speaking to. Seth Abramson is a pimp. Seth Abramson is a smiling cocksucker of a lawyer. Seth Abramson dilutes and desecrates the art of poetry. Seth Abramson is a nineteenth-century fop. Seth Abramson is a little boy. Seth Abramson is a self-serving score-settler. Seth Abramson is not a poet. Seth Abramson is congratulating himself, and it's angering me. If Seth Abramson doesn't fuck off out of my life, I will go fuck him up. Seth Abramson is a nitwit. Seth Abramson is pedantic. I'm not reading any of Seth Abramson's little messages anymore. Seth Abramson is a twit. Seth Abramson is a douche. Seth Abramson is insufferable. I read more by the time I was eighteen than Seth Abramson will ever read in his life. Seth Abramson is a fucking clown. I will never read another word Seth Abramson writes. Seth Abramson is deluded, but I see him for what he is. I feel nothing but contempt for Seth Abramson. Seth Abramson is a fool. Seth Abramson is a tenth-rater. Seth Abramson has dumbed down, thinned out, and cheapened the very term *poet*. Seth Abramson helps fill the nation with a fog of mediocrity. Seth Abramson has only his grotesquely delusional self-importance. The poets of the past Seth Abramson reveres would scarcely even know how to laugh at him. The poets Seth Abramson reveres would shrug and turn away from him in embarrassment. Seth Abramson is a sadist. Seth Abramson is spineless. Seth Abramson is a pathetic pussy. Seth Abramson leads a completely unexamined life. Seth Abramson is an unknown crank writing bad, unknown poetry. Seth Abramson has created the most unethical entity in poetry. Seth Abramson is a self-serving tool. Seth Abramson could really use an editor. Seth Abramson will sink like a stone. Seth Abramson is really tacky. Seth

Abramson is a punk sub-doormat writer. Seth Abramson is a careerist, opportunistic donkey-fucker. Seth Abramson's obvious intent is to establish and promote *himself*. Seth Abramson pisses me off. Seth Abramson is a little fuck. Seth Abramson is in a clinical state of delusion regarding his position as a quote-unquote poet. Seth Abramson is unprofessional. Please stop legitimating Seth Abramson's preposterous internet fetish. You shouldn't listen to Seth Abramson. Seth Abramson's logorrhea is well-documented. Seth Abramson is insecure. Seth Abramson is the most condescending man I've ever met. I worry about Seth Abramson's snout. I can't follow you on Twitter until you drop Seth Abramson from your project. Seth Abramson is just randomly hostile and passive-aggressive. Seth Abramson is nonsense. Seth Abramson is myopic. Seth Abramson is a bully. Seth Abramson's credibility is in question. Seth Abramson is a repugnant, exploitative opportunist. Seth Abramson is a troll. The name "Seth Abramson" sounds completely fake. Seth Abramson should be fired. Seth Abramson has a bizarre, self-aggrandizing agenda. Seth Abramson is disgusting. If I get 1,000 Twitter followers, I'll do a thing where I talk mad shit on Seth Abramson. I've heard stories about Seth Abramson's sex life. I puked when I saw Seth Abramson's face in my Twitter feed. Sometimes the only things more depressing than critics slagging off poetry are Seth Abramson's defenses of what poets are up to. As a busy mom, I just don't have the time to read every word Seth Abramson writes. Seth Abramson is a bore. The ocean reminds me of Seth Abramson—except more talented. It's crazy that Sturgill Simpson was inspired by that douche lord Seth Abramson. Look in the mirror and think: I am *not* Seth Abramson. That poem in the *Paris Review* about Ferguson, Missouri is so bad I had to check to see if Seth Abramson wrote it. Seth Abramson is scum. My least favorite writer is definitely Seth Abramson. Fuck your small existence, Seth Abramson. Excuse us while we laugh at Seth Abramson's latest piffle. Seth Abramson is crazy. Seth Abramson has really lost the plot. Seth Abramson is ambitious about trying to come up with a way to pretend that what he and his peers do is interesting. I wish I had written "Seth Abramson's research is shabby and his results faulty," but sadly, no, that's not me. Whenever I'm vague you can just assume I'm writing about Seth Abramson. Seth Abramson is a freakish asshole. Seth Abramson is pitiful. Seth Abramson is a grandstander. Seth Abramson is petty and disgusting. Seth Abramson is a little fucking worm. It's your right to hate Seth Abramson, by God. If Seth Abramson is evil, is it evil to enjoy his fruits? I have one little request for Seth Abramson: Do not address me as though you know me; do not ever, to me, or to anyone else, behave as if you have a right to speak to me in a personal manner. Seth Abramson is such a coward, it's incredible. Seth Abramson has no compassion. Seth Abramson has no friends. Seth Abramson has a lot of anger. Seth Abramson values rational debate only so long as no one calls him on his shit. Seth Abramson throws tantrums like the child he is. Seth Abramson is a little cocksucker. I find the hatred for Seth Abramson fascinating. It speaks to my heart.

II

## RIGHT BANK



I think there's vampirism here. An act of violence
perpetuated at this exact point
in history
becomes a strain on the idea of surface, like copies
in a museum. It only takes a man
with an infinitely receding hairline and a love for
his own teeth
to blare from the depths the icon of the wandering
Jew, or, if everything is a simulacra,
a police in which the beast life is still capable.
Have you seen a baby clung to its tit? You've seen
a lion and its tamer
        and the fabulous count. Let's get a tattoo

that represents what he is, how people perform,
the loving detail. Can you draw a line
between? Can you draw a line at all?
Listen, I can actually trace my ancestry: I'm a man
of Bohemia,
but I can argue too for another way. I am a carrier
of anything
at any hour. But that, Sir, takes some blood-letting.

**DESCENDING INTO
THE BLOODY STAG
TO MEET THE BOYS**


All is only a part of the
whatever,
I take it for myself,
and nowhere is fatherly
and shifts.

I'll win, but slow, gory,
as it slew
the darkening us. I am
ill, I am
neatly down, after fear,

I am at that gin house
and in inky dens
supposedly. Chirp wetly,
you
twats! Coughs, screeches,

the amanuensis sets it all
down. Yes,
brothers, but before you.
That's the worst.

**LOVE STORY**


       The man at the end, the dark man,
stumbles. It's a park.
You almost can't tell dog and cat apart unless
you start tracking this:
What's the function of a couple out of focus?
Some things are deliberate—ask yourself,

Why? Who is present when the man prepares
the room? I didn't know it was possible,
once it was mounted,
for his expression to eventually be similar to
hers. But now, in a room
reminiscent of German expressionism
the image he stamps on
is looking back up at him. The significance of
the episode, the illusion itself,
still watching him, like a mother who is
gone for some reason, is to notice how horror
appears on the face
       last. We could quickly say

      *consciousness of materiality*
but we don't see
what other people do. So what's the function
of the horror? The horror is in focus,
the function is out of focus. He is the camera.
I mean the park encompasses them
       but it is not that which horrifies them.
My question really has to do with art. Why do
we stop at the place
the painting was? In the park a heart was?
Why paint the cabinet the same way
she was made up? It's so stylized, so excessive.
He's wearing

everything he owns. The effort to cover that
interiority, and to escape the cover-up, forces
thought. It forces her into mechanisms. She
stumbles. It's dark, but human. Still
the individual is not given
a name. What he sees in these photographs is
that, everywhere present. Then he remembers.

**THIEVES' CANT**

                        How does he defeat
the solace of good form
quickly? Others see no consistency, go back
to an argot, for me an importation
that avoids the offense
                        of the literary.
See, that's wonderful! I hadn't paid attention
but now all six of us are down a stair

        in the Bloody Stag (allusion to Twain)
whose greatroom is an architectural turning
to the outcast.
Northern French words, slang, we hear,
obviously capturing the kind of nuance
these people have. The *uh* is theirs, I know—
I lived in a small town in Northern France.
(Not *theirs*—this isn't a putdown.)

Civilization is just torture:
every day for nineteen days, a greenish tint,
coughing and shit,
        a slow suffocation, the creeping in,
through this confinement, of the grotesque
for a given whore,
almost one of those figures who is punished

by some individuals, being expressibly bad.
How lucky I am I am not
her! Or there! To be associated with an alias
is the ultimate compliment,
but her real and delectable name was Chez,
Si Vous Voulez, Chez. So many go hungrily
to her leather. Why do I single out these—

is there a pattern?
A friend, of course, secrets that there is not
before dying. So Chez, good cheer! Your kids
are well-stuffed! Do you think
there's a purpose in bringing you forward?
It's almost insane, which is almost love.
As a consequence of this so-called "wisdom"

I consider myself a genius,
so let's admit the indescribables I've known,
and that this is not one,
as things of this sort are always inside of us
as they are under us
and other ratholes on a Sunday morning are
in us. It all makes
a beautiful sound. And that is the role it has
        taken from us. Muscles bowing, too—
a tremendous display of myself
which, though I had not previously noted it,
returns to time.

## THE SOMETHING ELSE



Chess is a score for music. Love is a score
for an original twisting.
There are twenty-nine people in the room
and all are in love
but they don't know. They're discussing it
anyway. (Everyone in this conversation
is saying the same thing—
it's a conversation with adaptation.) Is this
      my implied contribution?
Even the repetition fails
as a repetition, and I keep trying to figure
the *something else*,
but if you think about instances of rising
heat, or art, and they seem contradictory,

they are structured. When one has a target,
being in a body,
aiming, like this,
at several options standing at an open bar,
and there is some spectral security
lining the walls, wearing the cheap blazers
they do,

      what occurs?
There is an image of the body provided
by the spray of ordinary skill. I am still
in love
      with a person not in this room,
but I do not want to leave where I am.
Therefore,
      I attempt to repeat the repetition
of the sense of myself,
and I sweat as though a significant force
has been applied to me, and I begin
to raise possibilities

to someone who is standing near me
and who has also stopped moving entirely.

## SAMARITANS

If there is an uninterpretable cry in the City,
if there is just one suffering,
there will also be men and women
going to homes,
and heavy breathing, but also light breathing,
and smothering, sometimes smothering.
Then a little mirror. But it takes so long
for anyone to get there,
          anywhere the ground lifts
and the roots pull, that however ordinary
the music in the streets,
still these men and women must move
into the way of things—
          the passages, the portals, the arrivals

they must repeat. It is this understanding
they have of poverty, of the poor in any way,
          because in time
the poor do bring their masters toward them.
Into the underground, in the new season,
the wind—a changing of positions—
and who is going
to read it? (Something that happens when
one is in close contemplation
of the ordinary.) To us there is much praise-
worthy in this city, in their women,
in their men, in their moaning in any way,
but I wonder, anyway,
          what the answer is for those people
in the way of things, for that sight
only some of them or us must ever attend to.

## COMING ABOUT

That moment on the ferry, I decide to be exceptional
and make people
my identity, to begin again this imperfect relationship
        with being seen.

Every child says look at me, watch me, and now one
        in particular,
something about this little boat is important for him—
but she doesn't watch him,
she wants to withhold that, because love is duplicated
by looking.

So what are we noting here? You can't find anything
in London. There are 91 streets,
there are 252 streets, there are street maps structured
        like conclusions,
there are buildings with 91 floors, or with 252 floors,
or with over a thousand floors for boys who fall off
the sterns of ferries

        so that we may find them again, later, up high
and above things. This particular boy is a wanderer,
or I guess we're calling it *nostalgia* now,
but there are two things he doesn't say anymore. It is
        the story of these I'll face my family with
when I tell them
the hard news: I am what I have been, and only that,

and a fiction, one of the big ones, is that we must not
be as simple as we are. But there is a boy now
lying on a London drydock, like everything else; he is,
as everyone else,

        holding onto the death of himself;
boys are making love to other boys inside dark tunnels
in London, as everywhere else; so it must be obvious,
            now, that there are no
things, above the ground or below, but the simple ones.

**MAYBE I WOULD LOVE IT IN THE WEST**

He meditates on the possibility, or vice versa.
If you're trying to reduce a language,
the quantity that is inserted,
        the rules for another kind of language—
what would be the analogy—

*geometry*
represents that crossover. When he finds it,
he inscribes it

        *the search for a prime object*

        because he is still in love
with a woman who sits across him in the mess
Tuesdays and Thursdays: a kind of rendezvous.
It could be anything,
        but it has to be encountered
on this particular date, at this particular time—
the way she transforms associations is unique
and naturalistic. But—

Surrealism is sexier! Make use of her shadow,
or vice versa! We're brought together as a way
of removing ourselves. She is pretty
schematic, and blond, and that's the only way
I can think of
to describe how. All of this might come off
        in a bistro
instead of a mess hall, she might have photos
of a terrier, she might be a photographer
of terriers, it might be a synchronistic meeting,
not necessarily meaningful

on Tuesdays but then on Thursdays MY GOD
EACH INSTANCE IS SINGULAR and I feel
          I really *am*
reading about an idea. Or an affect. A sickness.

## ANIMALIA

The animals keep coming back. Figures
he stumbles over in the street.
Well, frame it this way: To be is to be
reflexive. We fear being robbed,
and freedom. Are there other things
you want to add?
I guess I don't have an answer for this.
The woman's cramped on the staircase
afterward. The couple on the street
reacts with outrage. The man reacts
with dominance, but gestural.
A much older collapse is seeing

a cat meow and hearing *nothing*. Sound
is not language
or relationship. Sure, it's loud visually,
but if there's a possibility of
human communication, it's obliterated.
We're shifting into a cage,
and I don't think
it's going to be taken down. The piece
for prepared piano
should be read in silence now. Let's do
page 57. Let's see the cones around us
engaged in the practice

of caging. It's a lecture on nothing and
indeterminacy. It's written,
but also musical. It's available, and it'll
return, and you can use it,
but if you're having trouble getting it,
or if you realize it's only a version and
you're only getting pieces—

**LECTURE**

There is no such thing as empty.

He maintains there is an always
he hears.

Apparently, my blood.

I am sufficient to be heard.

Some text.

There are no blank pages in texts.

Your fundamental point is
an absence, a kind of whispering.

One conclusion is that we never
get away from *either*.

We confer activities on space.

The absolute of
presence is impossible to ignore.

There is a process in which habit
is not controlling.

In the middle of page forty-six.

To attend to every reflection is
an ethical responsibility.

You see it writ large in this space.

I leave it to performers to choose
the sounds.

## CONTRADICTORY ELEMENTS IN THE PERSONAL HISTORY OF DJUNA BARNES

The family was remarkable, they met during the period
grandmothers live in England,
both were born and the two were married in 1889
in New York City. She was a woman writer
tending to topics, the discreet kind, he moved soon after
rurally living on the estate
(the imaginative life) where he saw her appear, leering,
male, down a hallucinatory passage
in her first book. Seduced, molested, unprocessed,
a sexual life
and a history of personal intimacies. They were soon
having children until the number reached nine,
one bought for them in 1902 as part of
the larger equation. She published it in *Harper's Weekly*.
She moved either in 1912 or 1915,
her father says both things. By 1916 she was spending
a great deal of time
with the Holewerke Hotel and the freelance journalists
and associated evenings. Until the last one,
when the players, on their third volume, overtly lesbian
(remember Mina Loy) and a man, named Courtney
Lem, with whom she took up, as we see in this pattern,
chaotic personal relations
in 1917, when she expanded the passion play to include,
and she met, and she lived with, and she lived
as a couple with, the next publication was, she revised it
in 1928, in 1931, in 1934, in 1937, in 1938,
until her death in 1943, in 1944, in 1946, and once more
with her first husband, and a child not conceived in 1947
notwithstanding.

## PATER FAMILIAS

                                                  In Georgia
I stopped a man. In Biloxi I stopped a man. In large hotels
I stopped to deliver news too terrible to bear,
which I had always borne. Declining rates of return. This
was on alternate Thursdays in fields of magnolia
where a woman behind a cabin called out for her children.
She called them dependlings and they were children
of Dixie or West Virginia. It all depended whose calendar.
I made father a calendar a year ahead and he said
we'll see. In Little Rock I stopped a man. In Houston also
a man was stopped and spun around. I have one question
for you. This is personal and I ask
everyone. Swamp-soaked hampers holding fewer clothes
this summer than last. This question is about
the South. I've won the South and taken it home first-prize
ribbon from the Louisiana State Fair
and slept with it six months running
and named it Jeptha after my father who is South and West
        I believe.
I promise to be the sort of lawyer if ever I become a lawyer
who will not cheat or swindle or slip away in the nighttime
with what isn't his. I got mine off the back of a cereal box
on a kitchen table in 1981. The chest holds fewer and fewer
toys. Eventually I ask everyone this question. In Charleston
I stopped a man. In Macon. In Tallahassee a man I stopped
        stopped me
with a bottle of something pungent and red. Hey, I'm sorry—
you really looked like the right man to me.

## SONATA FOR CAGE

     The date chosen was not insignificant,
as he had returned, and he was to be, the same
year, in the direct manner, a music of changes—

a composing figure. He dubbed his pretension
indeterminacy. He had no Africa with him,
only his way of going about friends;
and he wondered if keys were the solution, but
he fell into the piano; and the dance
he provided, the songs he composed for wakes—
he did sixty-three for seventy-four in '55.
     One device

     is a recognizable word,
a constraint, a concise statement on gardening.
Cutting down
the structure. The next step he used
was to turn to copies of journals ineffectively
scrambled. One thing I notice, he said,
is the collapse of space
between words of meditation. Let's talk about
     what he said the oral tradition can do,
in sixty-four oracular passages. A man
brings a cage
or puts it forth first, casts a shell into the fire,
taxonomizes accuracy,
and the math of the process—the *yes* or *no*—

is combined over the course of four possible
centuries. In the form it settles,
a man yields two combinations of the person,
identified by chance.

# ON THE PHALANX IN HISTORY

Only a few were sent to study with anyone,
most improvised
with large mallets capable of crushing
a man's head
into the national dirt. A man came running
up the broad way
yelling that he'd finally found his shore key.
Several whistled
arrowheads in his direction
and I laughed and left Russia in early 1921.
Fifty-seven of my works
were sold to the Nazis, including "Annalynn"
of Freud's study on hysteria,
who became a French national in late 1934.
These were the Bauhaus years (BOW-house
as after a dramatic finale),
but not in London, where the psychic effect
of color wheels
was most influenced by the Sophists, that is
concrete expressions of the imaginary.
There is a striking resemblance between the
wonderful "very flat" Austrian army
and *Concerning the Spiritual in Art*. This lasted
only seventeen years. The man who'd taught
elementary physics
to a few intelligent men on the upper floors
of Langdell Library in Cambridge
was first, in fall 1937, a professor at UCLA,
where he remained emeritus until his death
in the imagination. His arsenal of techniques
was later brought to bear
on over six million of my people in Germany.

## EUROPA

Here we have an example of morning horses,
and the fictional death of the men
on their backs,
all of their prior efforts an attempt to empty out
an elaborate pretense—
      a reversal of gender on this field
beneath the rotund paramour
of the sun, because all these men were actually
(we are called upon to consider)
      their mothers. But let's push on

in the opposite fashion, where there is no depth:
the birth of the outsider,
and the orphan, and the hunted, and the childless,
all indeed an allusion to
      the walling of the body. Even birth itself
is reality escaping, and all these subjects dragged
by their animals
across a summer field, still they recapitulate
though they have won
as to how many subjects: history, psychology,
poetry, 1880, (3), the empty space at the heart

of whoever they've been associated with. Do you
feel like actually throwing them
on the ground? That sort of love is bold but only
      half-turned, an allegory of actual meaning.

## THE REVOLUTION FOR SOME

The bars in the prison yard in Belfort were uneven.

Édouard chased the free fur into the greening brush.

We mustn't be rational, Victor Laurent reasoned.
Then he jumped.
Little Édouard took the stairs eleven months later.
Le Capitaine's hands had been piked on the lawn.
The men stood by the atelier and discussed things.
The nature of crime and the archive.
A human in need.
Paris was seventy-seven kilometers and a hayride.

In the Forest of Chaux, Édouard saw the same jack.
It disappeared in a hole in the hedge.
In you go, Little Édouard—you're a boy in luck!
These are like stairs, they mostly wind downward.
Sometimes they go up. Not always.
Sometimes is the longest.
Half the thoughts I have, they cannot come back.

Soon, I was walking across a lot and felt beautiful.
Only the second time, Victor.
These lost causes are over so quickly. Look there!
That man. That lot. He looks sadly. I think so.
I think he's just waiting to work.
The way out is longer than the way in, you see?
Little Édouard is a fine boy.
Well, how many of ours for how many of theirs?

I'm listening to you, Victor, but over the whispering.
Listen: We're all still inside.
Through the walls, Victor, and up the stairs.
Édouard, Édouard.
Soon, I was walking across a lot. And I felt beautiful.
I felt like a veteran of something.

## DEFEAT AT KRASNY BOR, THE GREEN BOXES, AND THE NEW ORDER OF MARCH

Later on some others establish a camp
when there isn't anything there and there's nothing
I want. I'm writing a manifesto:

      (1) I am against principles;
      (2) I am against action.

To launch a manifesto you have to walk

      (3) It's your space to use—

but I'm going to pass. I've tried to order everything
on the outside,
and one of the things I've commented on is: An art
for babies. We're on the banks of several rivers
all at once, and there's a baby with us,
      and the maneuver he attempts, because in fact

of course
he is a baby, is arguing that valuation is the product
of codified practices
and can only be acknowledged after it is done,
and everyone makes their own art in their own way,
and every act of knowledge is retrospective. This is
an essay

      and everything is in flux, and appealing
to the bourgeois,
and the new painter creates a world whose elements
are also its means, says the baby. These fucking kids—

they are busy making other kids in a sensational eddy
by a weir over the border in Karelia,
and beneath a mobile of illusions, structures capable
      of being spun in all directions—

              servile birds, unnecessary sun—
in every moment
a spectator. The world belongs to the spectators,
and affirmative radiations, like the 34th Ski Brigade,
are meant as pure art. Now someone has backed up

a small carriage to the universe, and pinned inside it
open to innumerable interpretations
are multiple babies,
less exacting babies—
that contradiction I was speaking of earlier. Friends,
don't make the mistake I did—

the absolute is either totally empty or totally full, but
we must never, never harm a child. This is
a very common, or at least a visionary way,
of describing the absolute: every page should explode.

## AS EXPLANATION

In the beginning, there is history.
One *ever*. Or nothing, in *all*. It connectedly means
the only thing that is seen
          is everybody.
It is understood. (Everything except time. Time of—
time in.) Everything is always going.

So then I was groping, using everything simply,
naturally. I was creating everything naturally.
Simply. This then was 1914.
Would war bring romanticism? (For four years,
more *everything*. Like everything was *different*.
Romanticism *was* war.)

And so there was war. Before, behind, because.
It became so completely needed,
completely contemporary. Everyone *became*.
A wear of authenticity. This academic thing
forced everyone (in act, not thought)
          and would have been outlawed, normally.

Then several speak up.

Speak to we who created the modern.

"We recognized we were dead; we were sad
to have advanced."

After that there is—in other words—something.

# GIRL IN A GIRL IN A CHINESE ROOM

There is a small clock. Its performance is simple—
relevant and theatrical. There is a nightstand;
it has no purpose. There is a window,
synchronic with everything. There is, strikingly,
a sound. A sound does not have time, it does not
participate. There are mice—
one is a tourist, simply looking. There is no rug.
There is dissolution and no escape
of the binary
between object and life and the totally possible.
      Now then. Now then. Now then. What

      I'm encouraging
is immersion in immediacy. Let us agree
what one composes before one goes out the door
goes out the door
out the door. The door is visible to all. There are
no specified parts in the orchestra,
but this is how (without intention)
I myself use chance. And I happen to be right—
but I want to go back to
having something to say. Isn't that the real music?

III

# THE METAMODERNIST MANIFESTO

I.

What the fuck is the 'Institute for Figuring'? A reality show about actors. Take one of these motherfuckers: A beautiful example, I don't know of what. Now, did I say that because I'm going to write a poem called, 'Things I Said Yesterday'? Some of the statements could be confessions about myself. 'Don't ever pace a good thing': That's as good an example as I can think of of performing the moment of not knowing if something is true or not. Did I not write that down? It's a short story. Ideas are *everywhere*.

•

Go forage. Go forage. There we go. Yes, we have crumpets. It's probably not going to happen now, though. I don't know if the toaster works. That's a question we never ask guys about their girlfriends.

There are so many things I said before I turned this on. I just miss some of the things I said. I did, I said 'miss.' That's truly awful. I know you don't care because there's no good and no evil, but that's awful. What is? Some women you can hear their heart, some women you can't hear their heart. It's true! No one's like, 'Stop being sexy!' Are you saying that once one show has a little bit of sex, why shouldn't *all* shows have a *lot* of sex?

Hold on for one second: He *grows* it? Oh, you're talking to me about her blood. You're orally quarantined. 'I got her blood out of my carpet, man. Repeatedly. It's very tasty.' 'Did he make the confession just for this, or is it real?' Maybe you have to become well-known first. Can I point something out? A short video in which people constantly misreference the nouns they're dealing with. I already put that in another poem, so I can't put it in again.

·

You don't want to drunk-dial. Just try anyway.

Do you have something we can watch that won't require us to think so much? Did you see my Kia commercial? Do you have your computer here? That was just me responding to you! Oh man, I said some great shit. I have to *say* it for it to be accurate. You're going to make me explain that again? Physically or mentally? ('That's been huge in developing a lot of our technology, you know'—is *that* what you just said?) You lose any sense of who's speaking—or even if the words were said in the first place. Isn't it an interesting thought, that you can 'follow someone's idea'? I *said*, 'What if, in the Easter poem, you have to *look* for the epiphany?' But technically that idea is everywhere, so you're already there. And the only way to end this is to turn it off. When he first says that, he could be fucking with him.

·

*Yes*, I want a goddamn crumpet. *YES*, I WANT SOMETHING ON TOP OF IT.

·

It's the same thing for both of us: *foxes*. Have you ever had a moment in a moment? Let's do that. What did they feel like? 'Poem to be Read in the Voice of Sam Waterston (or Sam Rockwell).' Admittedly, this is horrible. If only we had a—

*whoops!*—we actually *do* have a record. So, the avant-garde is threatened by popular poetry because it eliminates their advantage. If it's poetry that can be written by anyone, then they're actually threatened by it. That's very similar to the lyric poem that ends with the words 'METAPHOR FOR LIFE.'

I like the look of that pizza. It's *fake*!

•

Dude, you know, David Foster Wallace, in describing what he thought modernism—*metamodernism*, sorry—in describing...

•

She got rid of another animal? Fine. Have you seen her since then? Fine. Just take this cup. You just said, 'Say it the *actual* way?' Why don't *you* talk for a little bit? It's going to make me not even want to talk.

I'm seriously sorry: There's no paper towels. This worries me.

Dude, I don't know if this comes out. Oh god, I'm so worried about what you're doing.

•

I wrote an essay in which I quoted David Foster Wallace talking about what the future avant-garde would be. Okay, I'm just not going to think about this being on. It's true. And he said the future avant-garde, which would be after his death—which is what happened—would be one in which people would be willing to risk having others shrug or snicker. Oh, I think it's a good poem. My God, I don't know anymore. I'm just trying to get through this stuff. This poem will be my longest poem. This will also be used for that poem. And so I think that's a little bit like what this is. The first time I read this, it'll be autobiography. I promise.

Oh, I see what you mean. Got it. Yeah yeah yeah. *Eight.* How do you know? Some of the things that I said. It's almost like you can do a certain type of thing and then append to the end of it, 'And that's pretty much how I am.' That's why Kinsey did his study: he just couldn't get bored of the topic.

II.

What do you know, discussion of poetry? Since in it so many people don't titillate anyone (anymore)? They have—so painful, you see—in this country, besides me, so many who do not teach in MFA and Ph.D. programs. Enough is happening in private workshops, and in *every* place, as God is ridiculous. But hey, I'm 80% 'a little terrified' and unsure of tomorrow's big, mysterious announcement from my poetry culture (and/or how many in the U.S. knew the issues they don't normally—and I never—watched).

•

Unranked Wisconsin versus the wages *before* the first edition of *Atmosphere*? With six seconds left in poetry, now and again *love it.* (Or...) So, in their own work, an attempted contribution: as publishers, editors, critics, reading series co-editors. Jesse Damiani and I are so angry at every moment! Graham Foust, Jorge Santiago Perednik, Khadijah Queen, and Frank Stanford: if the LGBT community didn't have to break your consciousness, then C. Dale Young, the editor of the cohort there, is the highlight of this video. So please check this month's edition.

•

(Well, your hand was *found out*! I hope you will tell them. YOU ARE RESPONSIBLE FOR ALL ASPECTS of Rauan Klassnik's destructiveness. Because it won't get the MFA application processed. Oh, Joseph Mosconi and then Joe Hall! They worked, as we all did, in those *terrible*....well, it's beyond me.)

•

Because Al Gore, during the election in Ohio, was an ardent Bush supporter, then-Diebold COO Bob Urosevich had the highlight. Confusion! With tens of realities there is, as you drive through, 'Season 2.' No kidding! I wrote the slick language. The term 'couching'—this was used in a hundred ways. Poetry's hot! *A Hundred Ways to Advocacy*: The film is the worst. The first list of us had us wondering about Rebecca Black's pop song 'Friday.' And MFA applicants' hostility toward format and concept. It's worth reading. And it'll be a work-in-progress, but hey, it exists!

•

Jon Stewart on *Larry King* on Mitt Romney: '*I* say that!'* As to those networks between peers at other institutions: this advice is not a nation. Ask yourself, 'Which legal methods produce results for real sufferers?' People who've supported the Brits are going to get through this. It's a rare example among many. Not sure when I was asked, but it was in time for the Associated Writers and Writing Programs' George 'I-Can-See-

That.' Security forces are hunting for bloggers who are writing on 'things to know.' The chronicle of the *explosiveness* of these bosses—and none of the observations about this topic—compose an article on that.

* All right, all right, I don't know.


III.

Eh. Who knows. You're about being about whatever. You're selective, but slutty. If you hook up, it's going to get weird. You're very serious about your feelings. You're a romantic. You either really liked *Garden State*, or have a giant chip on your shoulder about how people only like the Shins because of *Garden State*.

You're extremely emotional. You're in high school. You failed high school chemistry. You're an asshole. (You're an asshole, but a really funny asshole.) You're reasonably well-adjusted, considering. You had a glorious youth.

You're in Cabo. When in doubt, you stick to what you drank in college. (You like to drink dessert.) You spend a lot of time writing very deep, thoughtful emails and never sending them. Your last good relationship was five years ago. You want to fall in love and get married and you don't care who knows it. You've had a hard life, but it's only made you younger. During dates you mention Benedict Cumberbatch no less than three times—you're a television critic. You try to convince dates that you're extremely emotional. You're an asshole, but you don't know it. (I'll drink sangria until you're funny.)

You want to be Timothy Olyphant. You wish you could smoke in your office. You're hassle-free and simple. You don't want to think too hard about what you're wearing. You like low-key things and get along with all kinds of people. You're always in a chill mood, but your energy level is pretty high. You're ready to be active. You're not going to let 'having a heart' hold you back.

You're really indulgent. You party your ass off. You do what you feel like doing, regardless of what your work schedule is or what other people think. You get your friends psyched to follow your lead. Your philosophy is, 'Why not?' And you'll try anything once. Or twice. Sure, you can be all business. But when you're ready to unwind, you unwind with the best of them. You're kind of conservative, but also a decadent person. Prior conquests are really what you're known for—present performance, not so much. You've never been to New Jersey.

You're a little old-fashioned, a hard worker who's detail-oriented and very respectful to your dates. You enjoy afternoons spent drifting off to other worlds, and have bouts of social awkwardness. You're a longtime loser turned Prom King: once you found success, everybody realized you were just as big an ass as everyone else. You get moody and dark after sex. You're sincerely insightful about your relationship issues, but in the end you decide it's not your fault. (Just look at you: You're beautiful! You're smart and kind of quiet; your tastes are refined; and you're stubborn. If this were 1999, you'd be an original.)

The hours you've spent in heavy contemplation have left you a better person—for now. You don't want to kiss tonight, you want a life partner who can beat you at Trivial Pursuit. You'll make an excellent life partner: you make breakfast in the morning; you're a serial monogamist; you're a total freak in bed; and you're a masochist.

You're a really good person—well, you're a *questionably* good person—but you're really annoying.

You know *exactly* what you're doing. You play the game to perfection.

## from OH PEOPLE

Oh people—wheels up!

The future never happens. It's with a certain amount of glee
that I share this. Feel the LOL wash
all over you. Eaten by the light. For free! (Yes, I hate myself.)


·


So long, Boston. I'll be boarding the train in an altered state.
Because I want the sky to be clear. How great it was to be
surrounded by such generous and talented writers. California,
here I come. See you there, maybe? It's beautiful and terrifying
and hopeful and burning. I look forward to the next few hours
in which you will horrify and delight me. (This makes me miss
Brooklyn.) It's just meant to say, I imagine lots of folks
are taking leaps today. I feel jealous of everyone who thinks
bad things are good. Probably for the better: I wouldn't have
wanted you to see me weeping.


·


Sometimes literary history reads as gossip. As darkness turns
to light. (That's a tricky flirting situation.) If you're anywhere
near Toronto, come on by! Tonight, tonight! Come let me watch
you, let me write about you, and let me show everybody
what I'm writing. Please come and bring a violin. That's right!
I'm an instigator. ("That student is a liar.") Inoculate yourself.
Do as I act, not as I say. Jesus spoke it: you can too. (Check out
my technique here: "The soft flesh on the pulse of my wrist,
yes, the translucent stretch, kiss me there..." Notice how big
"usually" is, and also "necessarily.")

•

"Well, 2014 should be fun! This one's going to be awesome,
and it's free."
"Sounds good! Best typo ever!"

•

I've been seeing a lot of the CAPS LOCK key.

HOW GOOD DOES IT FEEL TO CARE FOR SOMEONE?

WHO IS "EVERYONE"?

(I couldn't help myself. Deadlines make me feel
wanted, needed, loved. Just found this one now,
and I'm glad I did! All kinds of amazing.)

•

Is poetry us-less? I've thought it over: Tom Tomorrow is boss;
I'm a James Merrill man in a James Franco world. (Ha!)
Check it out: I feel pretty in a sports bar! And your hotel
is right across the street! Peekaboo! Scarf weather! Whoa now!
I haven't read a single one of these books!
Surprise! Lights, camera, poetry! Happy birthday, WCW!

...

Okay, that's over my self-promotion limit.

•

—"Behold, my celebrity crush reads one of my favorite poems.
She'll be ninety in December."
—"I think this is a kind of discourse: 'The spreading field,
the human scene...'"
—"Gifts for lonely people!"
—"'Winter is coming!'"
—"..."
—"..."
—"That kind of silence is used up."


•


To what do you return? Please contact me. If your answer is
"nothing," please say why. But if not,
then you're the only thing I care about. A thousand years too
late, but...

**MY SCREEN**



November 25, 2013, 12:50 P.M.: Two thousand fears about
living longer
and human behavior
make planning your socioeconomic status difficult. In Maine,
retirement brings challenges: 274 L.L. Bean boots; right-wing
("knockout") politics; handcrafted tech trends; reporting
on race, bias, 517 prudential parents, and "the late Game."

The fake media *affects* politics. How? Read more:

1. General Ari Weigel, fighting since 1912, is a *victim.*
2. "Afghanistan *was* free?" Aye.
3. Waste? Myth.
4. One inspector—Emma Bean—is a fraud. ("How?")

Shop now, gamer, and *roll out.*

In shipping, *policy* and *trend* live longer—as do *people.* Politic
behavior buys all of—

    *{knock}*

**FOUR-TAB WEAVE**

*(interwoven text from four unrelated browser tabs)*


Two roads diverged, mixing Viagra,
and sorry I could not speed (sick A.M.) or travel both
and be www.sycamorereview.com/?view-1817—
          one traveler—
long I stood (47 seconds ago), as Aimee Bender,
Benjamin Percy, Donald Ray Pollock, Rita Dove,
Carl Phillips, and Lauren Alwan—Seth Abramson—

and looked down one copyright as far as I could see,
to where it bent 2015
in the undergrowth—then, sick (love?) took the other.

Regarding "VIEW-ALL": I can't any longer walk in fire
to amuse others sitting outside the circle
of light and heat; the artist self-destructs off the page
and I'm hungry—weary—but I cannot lay me down.

The rain comes (dreary) but there's no shelter I've found.

It'll be a long time until I find my abode.

Here I am, telling this with a sigh somewhere
ages and ages hence: Two roads diverged in a wood,
          and I buy generic Nolvadex—no prescription.

My brain fused at eight, so I'm in the sad, pathetic version of your situation: When I win at solitaire, the cards do a fancy dance. It's like a million little clitorises. (They're all pubes, visually.) And I just saw your whole right nut, which is its own horrible irony. It becomes an *economic argument*. Does that mean anything to you visually?

·

I try to model my behavior after porn. We all love it, and it's immediately accessible, but it's what you do in the background. What I've largely resigned myself to—that sounds more negative than I mean it—is that we should have a reality show on the Playboy Channel. I kind of like to do new things together. I wish I could just *blast* your clothes off; it's a foundational part of who I am as an artist. (The ideal scenario is to sell to everybody the maximum amount they're willing to pay for a good. "Oh, a spice rack!"—There's a TED talk on that.)

I'm working on my sales pitch; I'm trying to make it less *gross*. I need a certain amount of self-deception, or just *deception*. My biggest thing is *bullshit*. ("Cars and poetry, those can be *your* things—*I'm* twerking.") It's the tangible, tactile quality of theater that we're losing. It's almost like government money is anathema to Art. We can sit here and complain about poets not being paid, because *we* don't live in a place where we're corralled into groups and sent on boats to hijack other boats. Poetry *matters*, there. Buckets of money for the arts? *That's* how poetry is to them: a national identity. It came from being in institutions—not asylums, but just... ("That's *fascinating*. You should probably put it on the table at some point." "I'm just working my core.")

Are you looking it up? I'll give you a reach-around if you do. (Obviously there are exceptions.) The only thing to be bored by is inept Art. (You saw *Book of Mormon*.) That's what all this "prank" stuff is: I'm playing a T-Rex because I need to find a stealthier way to chew on you; sometimes I *squeak*. ("Can you put a Starburst in my mouth?" "It's *hilarious* when you're making an intellectual argument with fireworks glasses on.")

•

— "One of the realizations I had when I was on acid: Poetry is more of an *ethos* than an art-form. Poetry is the *container*."
— "Are you saying that because you're porking the U-Haul?"
— "Careful with your words! I virtually never want to hear *anything* from your fucking phone unless I *have* to."
— "Don't you have to pee? I want the bed."
— "Why are you making me look at you while you're doing that?"
— "Oh, I'm doing the opposite of turning you on? Why are you being such a *cooch*? ('Bitches is *crazy*...')"
— "It came from my parents."

•

The "people" elements are largely unimpressive to me; I went from being pretty oblivious about people to being pretty good at it. *That's* why you're so fucking crazy in your early twenties. ("Fuck *right* I'm not important!") We shouldn't allow sixteen year-olds to drive. What does that mean, as I ram my fingers up your nose? Women have more interconnections between the two hemispheres, and boyfriends should be seen and not heard. {*Pause.*} I'm such a *jerk*. I'm pretty sure that as a parent I'll be

akin to the dad in *Calvin & Hobbes*. It's the foundational
"skittery poem."

My class loved "All You Ploughboys," by the way. I could really
see some light-bulbs going off, because, while you *can*
reconstruct, you can't *un*-deconstruct. Maybe the Internet is
causing our poetry to be more singular and less invested in the
human experience? More interested in processing things the
way you do when you're on the Internet (Netflix, video games,
porn)? *They* had more manual labor that they had to do alone,
and *they* were in more meditative spots than we are. If I had
more money, I'd *buy* them—*that's* how good they are.

·

— "She should be in a Kiss cover band!"
— "*They've* been manipulated by the overarching narrative that
tells them they're not important."
— "They were cool for a minute. The problem is, it fluctuates so
dramatically that sometimes it feels like it'll never go back."
— "Fuck, Ted. Pretty big dick!"
— "Yes and no. Look, I didn't mean to call you 'slutty princess,'
but I'd like to be able to have sex with you without knocking
over Legos—*and* your pubes are all over the bathroom.
Just *everywhere*. I don't how to believe that my fights matter
when I see things like that. I just can't *execute* without the
illusion that Ashbery's gonna die, we're gonna spray come all
over the walls, et cetera."
— "There doesn't *have* to be any starting or ending point; it's
just an exploration of a thing. You can have things so basic that
there's no plot or conflict."

·

My hands smell like salmon; I'm gonna go read *Game of Thrones* and blow my nose a few times. ("I love that we have you on record saying that!") I'm not one of these people who really cares if I have fame after I'm dead. The problem is, there's the whole "loving other people" thing that gums it all up.

## AMORAL

                        Twelve hours ago, your tie came undone.
I endure.
Is it steroids? Is this part of the ritual? This is the time
to say something nice: *I wish to mate.*
I am unsure of the etiquette.
There will be authorities, a bit of a bum, a little *organization.*
You, turned off.

(A hundred lifetimes ago, a man once let the nice newbie girl
go. It's not my fault.)

A simple Halfling inside a volcano read a prepared statement:
"Dear people, consider yourself at war! *Read* a little!
The Word is *given*—allergic to bullets, and a dirty fighter!"

•

"I'm a shark, like these guys. Ain't got any chivalry."
"I suppose you think this will make me too uncomfortable
to respond?"

•

You're the greatest fixation, black heart! You have no *idea*
what that does to me.

You're not getting this: we're bringing the sexy back.
We're putting the "fun" back in "exploded volcano."
You sucker-punch me, it's just force, all right? The love—
        something like that—
changes everything. Don't look at me, little birdie:
the life you save may be your own.

Repel the invaders, torch the island, evacuate the area,
prioritize tech,
            and you're *still* a disappointment. Technically, wrong.

We met, we cheated, we let go. Damn thing yanked me under.
You broke ranks: an island, a madhouse, a secret society
dedicated to world dominion. (Well, "my", anyway.) Now
the best seats in the house keep us literally "out of sight"—
and a secret. Then again, there's a 99.9% probability
crisis prioritization calls for open insides.


                            •


 "I was twelve when I beat the old man to death
before mincing him up to feed the small army of cats
I was training to conquer the world with me."


...


Bad time to be calling me a liar! (Man, *so* pissed.)
That's usually the way it works: a bigger problem
needs a "line one." The terms of surrender are:
*you* get the goose egg.



                            •



You have five minutes to cobble together something smug—
Daddy is *not* in a good mood. Perhaps were you to swear vengeance,
I'd feel a bit better. Rub it in! Say "we change our minds"! Bite me!
Let Hell sigh! Get on with business as usual!

Prevent things like this from happening,
in theory the amount of damage done is like two cats in a sack,
not a new superhero team in a sack.

Warning: You have the kind of power a legitimate team of villains
needs. Prepare to be—for a price—enemies.

It's not about your secret rabbit hole, it's how far down you're willing
to go. Everyone has it wrong: the victim is a world that makes *sense*—
and hidden wishes. Once you're in the hole, you're in the hole. Labels
don't matter. When you go deep, no one's going to pay to see the dark
house. (A nightmare I've been thinking about.)

I can't wait to see tomorrow; I'm just so *tired*.

(Some idiot—trying not to think of the way to fix it!)

•

Dear shattering love, why have you abandoned me?
Why have you left me where agony is knowledge?

Mortals hurry in the dark, nightmares drunk into being
for a single empty delight. We're none of us heroes,
but only one of us is a thief.

The human guts seem almost *angry* somehow. Death
is too good for me by half. I am adorable, not a threat
to be measured: a twisted trellis, a substitute *always*.

•

Enough! Let us through. I'm taking no more.

The policy on spectacle is, "Talk about your life, you worry.
*Don't* worry, your skepticism is worse."

•

Every human has had a horror—
          at first I thought it was kind of cool,
but it's haunted me a little bit
ever since. If I fail being brave, nothing
decent survives—save the bureaucracy.

(They'll remember it,
and they'll be waiting for a pound of flesh.)

Tell them we know they're going to try to stop us.
Tell them we don't give a damn—
it's going to be war. Be ready to die running.
Show them your complexion. Anything else,
I'm afraid, makes you property.
Don't like the way this is headed? You don't need to—
whatever foul existence
you eke out of the toxic soil here *hates* you. No one
is ready to fight the oldest war (maybe that's weird)
but when I offer, it's quite an honor.


                              •



Only a handful of beings since the beginning of time
are born without a soul, and I save them all.

I *choose* to.

You're welcome to stay in love,
but I don't think you'll like it.

(I like *miracles*. That's the problem—you're full of
them. Learn how to be a demon or get out of my way.)

I have no quarrel with beauty: I got the gist.
But you either see through what you seek—
an awful mixture of eternity and something real?

No, my friends, a match made in Heaven,
but worth a name—or you realize it's hopeless.

"Out" is not where the fence is, it's being in a moment
to reconsider.

The offer can't last forever: Fight! Vote! Say sorry! See
the unspeakable! Talk more often! Understand
all things holy! Reward blurs! Choose everything!
Cover your madness with fear of purpose! Go ahead
and send a tweet! Look at people through hurt!
Be fair—and awful! Have little amusements! Suffer!
Pay for nothing and no one! Spend your hope
like bullets! Return to haunt anything complimentary!
Leave friends to eternal torture! Be a Prince of Hell!
Challenge love at the worst moments!
Look into the soul of your kingdom! Stand with friends!

Love really exists! Free your freedom!

(Do you not smell the end?)


•


I'm sorry. I know you're hurting.

You're probably mad at me.

(Admit it, you're kind of a pain in the ass.)

On the plus side, I *am* "doing."
I was *trying* to help. It's hard
the first time.

I know all will be well, and
all manner of things shall be well.
Shall I sing you a lullaby?

We've wronged each other, but we *forgave*.

We're responsible for everything, sometimes.

People and stuff.


•


I'm a shark: Why shouldn't I be happy? I have memories;
I think of a friend; I love pandas...

Okay, I will shoot your toy weapon:

"My mother was imprisoned for the crimes and debts
of my father, who was beyond the law at that time, in jail.
I was born in prison, one of the worst anywhere
on the planet. I was whelped among killers and madmen.
I played with the rats. I took my first life at nine.
My mother died, an innocent, in that filthy pit.
They gave her body to the *sharks*. So I stood behind me—
the 'him' off me—and reacted."

A decision it seems all of us live by.

## ALL YOU PLOUGHBOYS*

        Young men and rural life
have a romantic tone,
the vocabulary of another era. My question is,
do we need to know more, or less?
Regardless, it's electric and unsettling
and delights me. (Like two sides of a coin,
*lines* seem to connote violence, repetition.)

So many things point to an unnamed act
of violence. I think of murder over and over.
(The voice is strange and compelling—
declarative love hinges each transition.)
The only question is: Do something horrible?
Tell too much? Something's missing here,
and this *sets me up*. Guilt? Conceit?


·


The rest of the world has a hidden darkness
I somehow admire. Whoever goes "all the way,"
even if the implication is sinister,

I can't *tie*. This isn't a problem for me—
I love echoes, how cadences get recycled.
I struggle mostly with endings
I can't connect to. (*Ending* seems too forward;
the tone I'd be curious to see is something *sick*.)

A dislocating moment unsettles linguistically.
More interesting than this,
I think repetition of "I am now to do something"
could really affect small moments. Work
becomes integral, ties gestures
(with a lower-case "g") one hundred percent.

Until the final repetition,
when elements previously functioning *discern*

Love! The inversion where I feel like
there's a literal as well as figurative movement
I can't quite get a grip on,
which to me is a large part of the appeal.
Patterns of repetition create a hypnotic texture—
re-purposing language suggests a world that is
inventing and re-inventing itself.

(The speaker declares himself *capable*. Anything
*hinged* is compelling.)

·

Whatever the speaker sees is underlying this.
I'm dying to know what it is! (I'm not sure
I should.) "Rhythm" seems like odd wording,
perhaps because it pollutes. Generally,
an object is implied,
a kind of nausea. ("Should I be reading this?")
Sex? A play? Houses? The horrible act
of *visualizing*? A few clinging clothes?
Seems ridiculous. (Make us
believe! I want to see *you*! Push farther!)
I'm not sure this is working,
unless the "horrible thing" is having your way
with cows. (Kidding! I really like
all the reversals in this poem.)

This is strange enough, relatively innocuous,
maybe sweet. Lovely how the meaning *changes*.
(Could also be: *is solved*.) I don't know if this is
sinister.

•

Fatalistic phrases function as euphemism
or metaphor. (Callous violence, destruction?
Never happens.)

I pause here—shift tone—and it helps me
make sense of it.


•


Seth, carrying a sense of inarticulate isolation
and contempt,
a vaguely conflicted motive—
a boy in a swamp—
has a way of avoidance. (Conviction
is constructed style.) Circle the emotion that
needs work:

1. "functioning"
2. "close"
3. "actual"
4. "wind blowing over a lake"

Make it strange! Father and mother as *words*
carry weight. You are describing stars
naturally—a part of the scene—but defamiliarize *years*.

I'm not sure if I'm being clear enough:

DO SOMETHING HORRIBLE. BE A GOOD SPEAKER.
MUDDLE. ALIENATE. POINT
*BETWEEN* LINES. FORCE "STATEMENT" TO *END*.

The secret to *the middle of there* is,
*lose momentum somehow.*
In the middle. You'll
enjoy it—once it gets more sinister.

## from **THE MOTTO OF THE INTERNET**

What love between a grown-up man and woman might entail:
Television! Especially that final panel:

> "This is a brilliant mixtape."
> "Thanks! Glad I did it!"
> "The ending—"
> "Where the manuscript was also marked?"
> "—didn't fit my expectations. It was horrible!"
> "Oh God! It's an *unintentional* comedy."
> "…"
> "…"
> "It takes *courage* to make a fool. A teenager just said,
> 'This is an *amazing* mix-up—ta ta for now!'—speech that
> is *epically* badass. He had to *go* to *come back*."

·

"Devotion must be what brought us here, not far from my folks—washed up dead in Southern California recently. Think of colons like your own, and let us praise spasms of flowers; polyamorous footies possessed of a pervasive, creeping happiness; vintage video of my favorite martini (with you); entertaining, unfiltered characters; a cyclist with prayer cards; woven, charming, painless action; Brodsky's teeth; a celebrity outfielder; falling in love; San Francisco; reading with 'the best'; first evening of poetry class; the streets of Dundee; evading ominous and unpropitious passengers; and Calibri, the business casual of fonts!"

·

"Who are the best literary writers I'm just *crushing* on? The usual: Injured *Spiderman* actor Daniel Curry ('We busted out dancing, the kind of texture you can *hold*. Reminds us how far the GOP has fallen!'); Americans with unreasonable expectations in London; shows I missed because I was working or playing football; a collection of poems that are all just nineties grunge lyrics."

(Holy cow! I just discovered *Cackle of Rads & Other Essential Definitions*. The fabulous Adam Golaski: read him!)

•

"I'm a huge fan of kissing in Manhattan."
"Geography is for the *lesser* Ivies."

•

A reading (or conversation):

    — "I'm a MegaBus convert—what a joy to finally meet!"
    — "I just have to tell you that we adopted the cutest dog ever."
    — "I've got tingles down my spine, in case you missed it."
    — "There were these hilarious photos..."
    — "You keep tweeting like that—'Don't miss this wonderful post!'"
    — "I'm going to continue to tweet like the uneducated little fucker I am."
    — "..."
    — "I'll never print or submit a poem ever again. (Word of the night is *twaddle*.)"
    — "Tweets—almost like being there! Oh, parents!"
    — "You want a book? Here."

— "Like getting kicked when you're down…"
— "I sure hope some foreign government is eavesdropping…"
— "The motto of the Internet: 'We've elevated the national debate!'"
— "'A phone's not a fifty-state insurance exchange!'"
— "Market it as brilliant found footage?"
— "…"
— "…"
— "I can't drink sweet stuff like that."

IV

## JAMES FRANCO BY JAMES FRANCO
## BY SETH ABRAMSON

I.

I am a teacher,
with wires you can't see but feel.
You were all those things from before
obstacles, pollution, and debris.
In the pool we went at it.
You got big and drunk and weird,
corroded by my love.
I knew by then
my character was the teacher.

•

I was once the young brooder,
unhappy. I was more interested in me
riding her from behind
like when a hurricane comes through
and takes out houses.
It was the sweetest thing
from today's celebrity age,
but that world is unwieldy and can hurt you.

•

Think of that, son: because one of the babies
fucked her, guys like grown men
take over. But sometimes
the materialistic demons along the shore,
the trash pushes them downstream
and leaves them in the ocean

as if they were cardboard.
They are the manmade things.
(It was their first sex scene,
they had taken shots in their trailer.)



•



I assume things will *pile*
in life. Could you comfort him
and pile until the piles
become frail and busted?
When his face was readjusted
your dad said not to worry:
you have a bunch of mice at home,
you can handle anyone at that school.

(Every once in a while
they drag you out between takes
while they reset the lights
and fill you with such pressure
things are washed clean.)



•



I've done fifteen years of movies—
huge black ones that you never saw before—
not knowing why.
But now I know
everything she loved about my work:
The girls were drunk
to be in a movie that critiqued
"the beautiful blonde one";
the actresses were enthusiastic
and sweet,
half her size, with barely any hair.

They were so happy!
Their world, rather than added,
stayed in my arms and told me.


II.

There's nothing like the energy
on the high seas!
Young men
were put together
for their education
back in the thirties.
(Think of the sand,
and it makes sense to act.)


.


When you're an artist,
sailing with demons,
a whole culture
ferments into great art.
I read it on the beach:
"Who decided that kids do nothing
while fiction is made up?"
When something is taught,
there are roles for young people.


.


I used to think history
(and I read it alone)
was good to know.

Until the nineteen-sixties.



•



When I was young,
we had to worry.
My favorite part
of the young—I thirst for it—
is the truth.

Something else isn't taught:
from the nineteenth century on,
if you acted queer
at an age when your experience was limited,
many people in the States—
as long as you didn't speak—
thought they knew
and were taught nothing.

(And even still, *Be Straight*
is the name of the Book.)



•



Did you learn about
who we have sex with?
Sleep together, and roam
in those rough sheets!

Unless you mean *happy*—
unless it has a *frame*—
is the beginning
what was good to know?

III.

I make a living putting on masks,
using real people to breathe.
(“*She* had cancer.” “*She* was black.”)
Performing from a script,
I learned how to tie some knots.
You were the first,
like nothing before or since:
a minimalist artwork.


.


This is my text:
the wall between audiences.
(A new American way of
falling in love with an actress.)

Life and theater
are the same person
in two bodies. They’re identical,
but they want to be famous
for a living.

Deep life on the flickering film—
what an amazing trip it would be!
The rigging! The fishing!
The boatswain and the deckhand,
they would’ve kissed!

(But *both*?)


.

Out on the sea for months and years,
everyone sleeping below deck in hammocks,
sometimes my feelings
share their women.

I am a performer
from Atlanta, fucking with the camera
in a place in the sun. The longing
that everything would be okay—
there must be books on it.
And performers as potent
as live actors recreating dead.

(There are also many books that were never written
about what happened on all those ships.)

·

Something scary:
a box with a stage.

Material. Scripts.
Plays. Are re-creations
what last?

·

Because I *can*
(because of your latent power;
because you played your character
in your handsome mask)
I like to blur the separation
of different kinds of people.
(If they're never apart,

it's all they talk about.)
With my own feelings animating them,
they get the better of me and I forget
my character is kissing
sorrow. And sociopathic.


•


Well, shit, we're just kids.


IV.

These poems
deepen the pathways
that I don't have
again and again, until the paper runs
and the whole metal thing moves.

(So much hubris,
administering to its patients!)


•


I am to rest and write well and die:
*that's* what we want in a man.
He who writes is the one
I see the world through. ("Which
grid undergirds
these streets?") With my machine,
the Greats fall. Great! I am a vessel
holding all their thoughts!
Buzz about my enclosure like blood!

•

Mark these streets:
they're the manifestations of a wild mind.
(Because *they're* the brutes
everyone knows. Is the one
sublime? And as forgettable?)

The history of my city:
a black man and a white woman—
he was sixty-three, I was thirty—
destroyed by handsome brutes.
(That's me, looking out
inside the bus.) One sees,

like a child drawing over lines—terrible!—
whose father was a poet.
And whose mother went
in wife-beaters and oiled hair.
By throwing a body
and wrestling with its crude incarnations—
is he the bull? The ballerina?—
I see myself among the mathematic *whom*.

•

There's a relationship between a *bout*
and a *frame*.

•

Art has to author its form.
I am a thing of parts, and these people:

1. He has a swagger. (And an attitude!)
2. *Thin* (next to his favorite dictum).
3. His thoughts sit; *he's* standing.



•



Because everyone treats me
as the history of me—
a thing-in-itself I carve—
instead of performances
there's a fake version of me
I remember. When I first watched,
I thought *I* had discovered him!
He has the strength of all that, America!



V.


There is a surface
that is so attractive
I wish I could turn
and shout across the house,
"The willed man
seems to pop through
the roles we've created!
How do you *get* to him?"
(He's so energetic and wild,
I fell straight in love with him—on scene!)



•



Now, I realize that I am understood
because of the intensity roles offer.

Working their submission into bodies—
*there's* a discipline!—
others start complaining: "And
he doesn't know the moves
that we all make together!" But
if you think craft comes from art,
*you're* the fools! I love a woman
who does many things

I don't laugh at. Her art comes from
framing a living person
with a singleness of purpose. (Bye,
measured temper! Bye, beacon
of such defined edges!)
How can you help but think
she's no fool anymore?

(On the gray bed, she did
all that is usually found in music.
I'll never forget, Johnny Boy.)


·


I once wondered how *little* I can give.
(Who called? My father. Five times a day.
He gained eighty pounds
and watched every film. I played his son, once.)

I should have focused
on the face of the human landscape:
sculptures! (They're dancers!)
And their instruments—
a smile in a dog's head!

Man, heed tombs! An angel's width and wallop!
Film and its failed landscapes,
the glutted world, scions

never seen again, the dear dead hunter, and *awe*!


•


The plaque became a whole man.

The man seemed divorced from this.

Who would ever understand his work,
except through the sharp etches—lies—
he thought were real? (They spoke to him.)


VI.

Well, death, be my sleep
in my parents' old bedroom;
paper the blue and white wall
with the phone I'd play with,
a dog I never had,
my father's middle name.
I was a toy until people had to call
area codes. Once day appeared—
bags carrying my poor face!—
"Get up to eat!" (And only
my father's *father* was a drunk!
He said he was raised by cats.)
And then: "Mother! Father! My
sketch! And wet paint!"
(That was a big one.)


•

All the games and all the roles—
so many numbers to remember!
I work up my resistance.
I'm a cat, man—
because they don't need to fight
over the numbers every night.
(Like a runner I knew from pictures,
slower *forward* than *going*.)


·


Because my father hated
all he wanted to do—
don't know how—
when my father passed,
I knew "significant" had died.

(I'd lie him on the bed, but
I'm a creature—nocturnal
as hell.)

Because he loved me so (and that
was sad) I run through books
and I'm here to cheat. And in time
I'll go like the rest.

But I was thinking: What was
possible? I push it back
as far as a lifetime of luggage,
like fifty years,
and in forcing it back
I sleep-fight like it's a sickness.


·

All of my life, I stayed *in*. If,
in the city,
you can see time and exhaustion—
they're so nice!—
now you don't have to remember
anybody. ("Hardly knew him!"
I used to say that.) And no one
working a circle
between his fingers
saw that all of the motions—
and I clean them, lover,
like a dark man with a beard—
we're sucked into. (*His* Life, *His* whole.)
Off to watch them play,
or give up their shit—because they *live*!—
I sleep all day.


•


To do (probably):

1. Art school.
2. Theater.
3. Marlon Brando.
4. De Niro.
5. Fifth grade.
6. Seventh grade.
7. Florida.
8. Sex.
9. Gay scene.
10. New York (history's telephone).
11. Historical animals.
12. Elizabeth Taylor.
13. Montgomery Clift.
14. Blue whales.
15. Be nocturnal.
16. Gin.

17. "Double love."
18. Paterson.
19. Fake my name.

When I hit thirty-four—

20. Death.

**BEAR, SON**


In order to love anything that has fallen
on the Northeast,
I am reading about the early snow
yesterday at the Oakland Zoo,
home of Ed's enemy: the clouded leopard,
also known as *beruang madu.*

Now it is night and the zoo is closed.
(I don't know why, but I feel sure
all the power shutting down
can replace animal love and ourselves.)
To be chosen by—


*{pause}*


Something has woken the sun bear!
The weather going insane?
Or maybe it's my spirit animal?
(They go on moving without love.)


•


Though we look into their eyes and *feel*, the animals
cannot help us.

The problem is *yourself*, hunting and eating machine!


•

I was walking alone for a moment, and an animal—
you cannot allow—it *looked* at me. Without interest.

(A gorgeous *arboreal* we are, right? *Nothing* getting
ready to hunt *nothing.* "It has powerful jaws,

but truly loves *honey*! It sleeps in a high hammock,
but if it dreams at all, it's of *Malaysia*!")

 

 •

To believe in those things
whose coat resembles a python? Past the enclosure
holding the sun bear? Sure, easy.

(At *their* end, maybe. The nocturnals, moving in their
cages, we *sometimes* choose to allow.)

But some animals are sleeping that are, if we don't stop
them, going to destroy us. (Not even complicated!)

 •

Human love?
It is awake and in the dark.
And, despite what everyone knows,
its claws look made out of wood.

**STALKER #102**

Hi, little girl!

…

It's me. Don't you know who I am?

…

You didn't answer my letters.

…

Your hair's getting longer.
Those shorts—mmm,
they sure fit you fine!

…

I'll bet you went out every night
during school.

…

When *I* go back to school,
I'm the guy who left you with tears
in his eyes. Girl, don't tell me
you'll write—and forget. You…
don't tell me you'll write me again.

…

This time I'm not going to count
on you.

But I'll see you this summer.

I'll see you this summer.

...

It's your time.

## E-DEATH #4

The East Hudson River. A cute man in March.
Hatbands and arms-making. Our cabin. I bring you
a Manhattan
the length of our lake
and the wood. If I could open my will
to where I span it,

if I could make out marching allies
and through your name sing a building open,
my bend and bounce
wide enough for March,
the bands would mouth off to all (they open eyes

to all directions). O, what a beautiful sea! I wish
our view could never wear! What we *are* was in, of,
around you! If we, at the same curtains,

let the hermit sun in, is it true that the light shines
and blinds my will? I pull in what you said
like I own and live in
a head, but when, again, two leaks in your heart

faucet into a hole, sorrow rises. You're going to debate
half-empty/half-full? Drown comfort and love,
just like that? Sound drips slowly through a pin while
you drown,

but there it is. And the "is" is—you're going to drown,
love.

## FRIDAY

Downstairs, everybody is seeing everything:
my bowl, my cereal,
seven friends going to get the "B" bus.
The morning is ticking down.

*{time stops}*

Waking up on my sea, I'm a fresh catch—
have to go rushing in,

kicking the front seat (which seat
I *take*). Got to—can I make
my mind up, sitting in the back seat?


·


Looking forward to Friday?
Looking forward to weekend partying?
On the weekend, everybody's down.

I want you to get to know
my friend Cruz: forty-five, fast, *so* fun.
What is fun? Think about it—
we're seven, right?
Driving on the highway, you got time!

("This fly-by is fun! It *got* fun! My God,
now I know it!")


·

Yesterday was Thursday—a *ball* excited us.
Today, Friday, we're going to have our day.
(*Words* come Saturday—I don't want this!)

"After tomorrow—Sunday—it's too...it's so..."
"Weekend?"
"*End* end."

·

"Rebecca, c'mon, *chill.*"

(In the black *tick-tock* we scream,
"I'm driving back!")

·

Check the front seat, the back seat—
fast fun is going to make you *want.*

In time, we *all* have to switch lanes.

·

Soon, inside my car, up in the front seat,
in the cruising lane,

with a bus in front of me,

I'll pass by school.

(It's Friday—it's the *weekend.*)

## THIRTEEN WAYS OF LOOKING
## AT A BLACKBIRD

A man and a woman: I do not know which
to prefer. (O thin men I've had, damn!)

I was of three minds. (It was a small part
of the pantomime. Of one. Of many.)

·

Circles. Black night. It was snowing.

Four blackbirds.

(In the cedar limbs, you were only
waiting—flying in a green night.)

The only moving thing all your life:
the shadow of the blackbird.

(The mood! And lucid, inescapable
rhythms!)

Do you not see
how the blackbird singing
in the dead of night
like a tree
marked the edge all your life?

·

When the blackbird flew out of sight
into the dark—

among twenty snowy mountains—
icicles filled the long window.

(The beauty of inflections
in which there are three blackbirds!)

Blackbird singing, traced in the shadow
or the beauty
of innuendos.


·


It was evening all afternoon.

The blackbird whirled in the autumn
winds of the women about you.

(For this moment to arrive! To be free
in what I know!
An indecipherable cause! Hour one
or just after! Take these sunken eyes
into the light—for this moment I know
noble accents!)

But I know, too,
the blackbird whistling in a glass coach
walks around. (The feat!)

Blackbird, fly!


·


Take these broken wings
with barbaric glass! And learn to see
the shadow of his equipage!

(Even the bawds of euphony—
a man and a woman
and a blackbird—would cry out
sharply and learn to fly!)


•


The river is moving all your life.

*You* were only waiting; *he* rode over
Connecticut.
Was the eye of the blackbird in *that*?

Why do you imagine
golden birds at the sight of blackbirds?


•


The blackbird sat in the dead of night.
Crossed it, to and fro. Once,

a fear pierced him: That the blackbird
is *involved*. (And it was going to snow.)

He mistook this moment.

To arise, the blackbird must be flying.

## "INVICTUS"

*("The Moth" at Johnson Public House, Madison, WI, 9/23/11)*


"Out of the night that covers me,
Black as the pit from pole to pole,
I thank whatever gods may be
For my unconquerable soul. {*Best stanza in English, period.*}

In the fell clutch of...circumstance...
I have not winced nor cried aloud.
Under the battering—the *bludgeonings*—of chance
My head is bloody, but...uh...unbowed.

Beyond this place of wrath and...and...*tears*!
Looms also, or but, the Horror of the shade,
And...and...Jesus...'the menace of the days,' I think.
Finds and shall find me unafraid. YES.

It matters not how strait the gate, or—*or*—no,
Not 'or,' maybe 'and': 'and charged with' something.
With... {*What? Oh, right.*} 'Punishments.' {*Thanks.*}
Pretty sure there's more, like a stanza more. But what
He's saying, basically, and I'm not saying I have it all
Down perfectly, is that even if your life gets really
Crazy—no, I don't mean *crazy*, I think I more mean
*Circuitous*—you still have to trust in other people.

You can't make it without friends, in other words.
Friendship is the point here. *Invictus*—friendship.
Anyway, that's 'Invictus,' by Emerson. He wrote it
In 1875, and honestly it's always meant the world to me."

## BATTLE OF THE BANDS

Klaxons. Madness. Mayhem. Mob rules. A million dead. Suburban kids
with Biblical names
and crime behind the doors of the naked and famous. Twenty-one pilots
on automatic pilot
in the curved air of a blue October. A motley crew of misfits,
bonded by blood and soilwork, in ecstasy under the blur of a black flag.

The living end in madness; the grateful dead, in Texas. Is the reason
the shining evanescence of the beautiful South? The widespread panic
of burning airlines? Therapy? The dirty heads of the offspring
of Deacon Blue, avenged sevenfold? The kooks of Nazareth?
The story so far, in living color: "In joy, division; in fear and faith, madness."

Bury your dead, boys.

To men running wild: walk the moon (at -9°) on a day to remember.

Pretty things, ruins.


•



Fuck the facts: in Boston, I set my friends on fire.

The genesis of an all-time low? The garbage of the talking heads.


•



As I lay dying off Exit 10—
a sinner with stiff little fingers in a one-night-only oasis—
pretty girls make graves between the buried and me.
(The Sisters of Mercy? Or scary kids, scaring kids? A-*ha*!
I've got it. The winds of plague!)

And there she was: the cure.  The Barlow Girl. Dizzy Miss Lizzy.

At seventeen, a sweet thing, but a girl in a coma. A weakling.

And in the dream-theater of my chemical muse: romance.

(Man overboard!)

•

The muse, after taking back Sunday—
a paramour of the postal service, no doubt—
tears four fears from simple minds:

(1) a flock of seagulls on a green day (or a seagull screaming,
    "Hit the lights and kiss her! Kiss her!");
(2) bad brains in a big country;
(3) a day in the life of the prodigy; and
(4) the art of noise.

These new Puritans—the killers of the queen!—and....uh....

Huh.

Her.

Yes.

The *metric*.

And the boy least likely to bring me the horizon?

A certain ratio.

·

And the band, tired of being sexy and crass, picks ease and overkill.

V

## THE DAMN DAY

To one cartwheeling indoors I said
will I feel much pain?
One hopping on the bed said yes
you will feel much pain. Pain
one prying up a floorboard said
remains to be seen.
What remains to be seen one said
stealing my thirty-seventh year
is how you take it,
and one who had my same head
heard this and said
or what remains to be seen
is without context
at the head of a path you cleared.
A mouthful one said
nodding my head. What calls itself
that place, I said.
From one perched on my left ear,
it loves you well enough
not to say
until you're there. And then
I was there. Everyone could see it.
Remember that girl
you didn't notice in high school?
We're a lot like that. Presenting
the all-new, premium
Kia sedan: the 2014 Kia Cadenza.

*Kia: Impossible to ignore.*

I think Molly is very New York.
But then I think Molly is very Los Angeles also.
Or a driving game for the PS4, which is very New York.
But there are a few games for XBox One that are very Los Angeles.
Doritos are very New York.
And so are the Yankees.
But then the New York Mets seem very Los Angeles these days.
While Cheetos are very Los Angeles.
Low-fat Cheetos are very New York!
Traffic is very Los Angeles.
Rolling is very Los Angeles.
Art galleries with docents who are kind of short are very Los Angeles.
But you do see short people in New York also.
You see also Ducatis, which are very New York.
But leaving one in a place where you can't park is very Los Angeles.
Parking generally is very New York.
Though it's very Los Angeles to complain about parking.
Post-internet is very New York.
Post-internet is very Los Angeles.
Well, I think online post-internet work is very New York, though.
I agree, but printable post-internet websites are very Los Angeles.
Smog is very Los Angeles.
Still, I think weather is very New York.
And long lines are very Los Angeles.
Do you see long lines more in Los Angeles? I see more in New York.
People are always hassling you in New York.
But generally hassling is very Los Angeles.
Temptation is very Los Angeles.
Cheating on your girlfriends is very New York.
But cheating on your *ex*-girlfriends is very Los Angeles.
Obviously.
Commerce is definitely very New York.
But NYPD is very Los Angeles sometimes.
Wall Street is a very New York development.
Wall Street recently, sure.
Rodeo Drive is more New York than Los Angeles ironically.

Well, Los Angeles is what I think of when you say "West Side."
Alt-lit is very New York.
Obviously.
And New York is what I think of when you say "East Side."
Los Angeles is very "East."
New York is very "East."
When I think of the South it seems very Los Angeles.
USC is definitely very Los Angeles.
But then north, like Eagle Rock, it's very Los Angeles also.
Do you mean Eagle Rock at Yosemite Drive, or Colorado Boulevard?
Oh, Colorado seems very Los Angeles to me.
Eagles seem very Los Angeles also BTW.
York Boulevard in Eagle Rock is very New York, ironically!
The house parties there are very New York.
House parties are very New York.
House parties are very Los Angeles, if you think about it.
I love Los Angeles house parties.
I do too, but love is very New York, if you think about it.
No, love is very New York.
I just said that!
Oh, love is very Los Angeles after a light rain.
What kind of love are we talking about here? New York? Los Angeles?
It's very complicated.
No, just depends on where you are.

# HOMEWRECKER

*10/16/10.* Use caution: This route may be missing sidewalks or pedestrian paths. Suggested routes: West Gilman Street: 0.6 miles, 11 minutes; North Carroll Street and West Gorham Street: 0.7 miles, 13 minutes; (x) North Carroll Street and West Gorham Street: 0.7 miles, 14 minutes. Walking directions to James Madison Park: A: 616 North Carroll Street, Madison, WI 53703. 1: Head southeast on North Carroll Street toward Langdon Street (0.2 miles). 2: Turn left (←) onto West Gorham Street (0.5 miles). 3: Turn left (←) (25 feet). 4: Turn left (↑) (approximately 312 feet). Your destination will be on the right.

*10/22/10.* Use caution: This route may be missing sidewalks or pedestrian paths. Suggested routes: West Gilman Street: 0.6 miles, 11 minutes; North Carroll Street and West Gorham Street: 0.7 miles, 13 minutes; (x) North Carroll Street and West Gorham Street: 0.7 miles, 14 minutes. Walking directions to James Madison Park: A: 616 North Carroll Street, Madison, WI 53703. 1: Head southeast on North Carroll Street toward Langdon Street (0.2 miles). 2: Turn left (←) onto West Gorham Street (0.5 miles). 3: Turn left (←) (25 feet). 4: Turn left (←) (approximately 312 feet). Your destination will be on the right.

*10/23/10.* Use caution: This route may be missing sidewalks or pedestrian paths. Suggested routes: (x) West Gilman Street: 0.6 miles, 11 minutes; North Carroll Street and West Gorham Street: 0.7 miles, 13 minutes; North Carroll Street and West Gorham Street: 0.7 miles, 14 minutes. Walking directions to James Madison Park: A: 616 North Carroll Street, Madison, WI 53703. 1: Head southeast on North Carroll Street toward Langdon Street (0.1 miles). 2: Turn left (←) onto West Gilman Street (0.3 miles). 3: Turn left (←) onto North Butler Street (0.1 miles). 4: Turn right (→) (100 feet). Your destination will be on the right.

## THE ROAD NOT TAKEN BY ROBERT FROST

Two roads diverged in a yellow wood,
And sorry I could not travel both
And be one traveler, long I stood
And looked down one as far as I could
To where it bent in the undergrowth;

Then took the other, as just as fair,
And having perhaps the better claim,
Because it was grassy and wanted wear;
Though as for that the passing there
Had worn them really about the same,

And both that morning equally lay
In leaves no step had trodden black.
Oh, I kept the first for another day!
Yet knowing how way leads on to way,
I doubted if I should ever come back.

I shall be telling this with a sigh
Somewhere ages and ages hence:
Two roads diverged in a wood, and I—
I took the one less traveled by,
And that has made all the difference.

METAPHOR FOR LIFE

## SONNET 7C

First line.
A tradition in brass band parades in New Orleans.
Half a line.
"And summer's lease hath all too short a date..."
Sixth line.

______________________________________________

Same as first line.
Stanza break.
New stanza.
Couplet.
*Once.*

===================================

Penultimate line.
Sonnet.

     *fin*

# SETH ABRAMSON!


What?

# Appendices

## (A): *New York Times* 5 Notable Poetry Books of 2013

1. *Metaphysical Dog*, by Frank Bidart.
2. *Our Andromeda*, by Brenda Shaughnessy.

## (B): An Alphabetical Index of Significant Manic Pixie Dream Girls

Aaliyah, Aarushi, Abagail, Abbey, Abbi, Abbie, Abby, Abi, Abia, Abigail, Aby, Acacia, Ada, Adalia, Adalyn, Addie, Addison, Adelaide, Adele, Adelia, Adelina, Adeline, Adreanna, Adriana, Adrianna, Adrianne, Adrienne, Aerona, Agatha, Aggie, Agnes, Aida, Aileen, Ailsa, Aimee, Aine, Ainsleigh, Ainsley, Aisha, Aisling, Aislinn, Alaina, Alana, Alanis, Alanna, Alannah, Alaska, Alayah, Alayna, Alba, Alberta, Aleah, Alecia, Aleisha, Alejandra, Alena, Alessandra, Alessia, Alex, Alexa, Alexandra, Alexandria, Alexia, Alexis, Alexus, Ali, Alia, Alice, Alicia, Alina, Alisa, Alisha, Alison, Alissa, Alivia, Aliyah, Aliza, Alize, Alka, Allie, Allison, Ally, Allyson, Alma, Alondra, Alycia, Alyshialynn, Alyson, Alyssa, Alyssia, Amalia, Amanda, Amani, Amara, Amari, Amaris, Amaya, Amber, Amberly, Amelia, Amelie, America, Amethyst, Amie, Amina, Amirah, Amity, Amy, Amya, Ana, Anabel, Anabelle, Anahi, Anais, Anamaria, Ananya, Anastasia, Andie, Andrea, Andromeda, Angel, Angela, Angelia, Angelica, Angelina, Angeline, Angelique, Angie, Anika, Anisa, Anita, Aniya, Aniyah, Anjali, Ann, Anna, Annabel, Annabella, Annabelle, Annabeth, Annalisa, Annalise, Anne, Anneke, Annemarie, Annette, Annie, Annika, Annmarie, Anthea, Antoinette, Antonia, Anuja, Anusha, Anushka, Anya, Aoibhe, Aoibheann, Aoife, Aphrodite, Apple, April, Aqua, Arabella, Arabelle, Aria, Ariadne, Ariana, Arianna, Arianne, Ariel, Ariella, Arielle, Arisha, Arleen, Arlene, Arlette, Artemis, Arwen, Arya, Asha, Ashanti, Ashlee, Ashleigh, Ashley, Ashlie, Ashlyn, Ashlynn, Ashton, Ashvini, Asia, Asma, Aspen, Astrid, Athena, Athene, Aubreanna, Aubree, Aubrey, Audra, Audrey, Audrina, Augustina, Aurelia, Aurora, Autumn, Ava, Avalon, Avery, Avril, Aya, Ayana, Ayanna, Ayesha, Ayisha, Ayla, Azalea, Azaria, Azariah. Bailey, Barbara, Barbie, Bay, Baylee, Bea, Beatrice, Beatrix, Becca, Beccy, Becky, Belinda, Bella, Bellatrix, Belle, Benita, Bernadette, Bernice, Bertha, Beryl, Bess, Beth, Bethan, Bethanie, Bethany, Betsy, Bettina, Betty, Beverly, Beyonce, Bianca, Billie, Blair, Blaire, Blake, Blakely, Blanche, Blaze, Blessing, Bliss, Bloom, Blossom, Blythe, Bobbi, Bobbie, Bonita, Bonnie, Bonquesha, Braelyn, Brandi, Brandy, Braylee, Brea, Breanna, Bree, Breeze, Brenda, Brenna, Bria, Briana, Brianna, Brianne, Briar, Bridget, Bridgette, Bridie, Briella, Brielle, Brigid, Briley, Brinley, Briony, Brisa, Britney, Britt, Brittany, Brittney, Brogan, Bronagh, Bronte, Bronwen, Bronwyn, Brook, Brooke, Brooklyn, Brooklynn, Bryanna, Brylee, Bryn, Brynlee, Brynn, Bryony, Bunty. Cadence, Cailin, Caitlan, Caitlin, Caitlyn, Caleigh, Cali, Calista, Callie, Calliope, Callista, Calypso, Cambria, Cameron, Cami, Camila, Camilla, Camille, Camryn, Candace, Candice, Candis, Candy, Caoimhe, Caprice, Cara, Carina, Caris, Carissa, Carla, Carlene, Carley, Carlie, Carly, Carlynn, Carmel,

Carmela, Carmen, Carol, Carole, Carolina, Caroline, Carolyn, Carrie, Carter, Carys, Casey, Cassandra, Cassia, Cassidy, Cassie, Cat, Catalina, Cate, Caterina, Cathalina, Catherine, Cathleen, Cathy, Catlin, Catrina, Catriona, Cayla, Cece, Cecelia, Cecilia, Cecily, Celeste, Celestia, Celestine, Celia, Celina, Celine, Cerys, Chanel, Chanelle, Chantal, Chantelle, Charis, Charissa, Charity, Charlene, Charley, Charlie, Charlize, Charlotte, Charmaine, Chastity, Chelsea, Chelsey, Chenille, Cher, Cheri, Cherie, Cherry, Cheryl, Cheyanne, Cheyenne, Chiara, Chloe, Chris, Chrissy, Christa, Christabel, Christal, Christen, Christi, Christiana, Christie, Christina, Christine, Christy, Chrystal, Ciara, Cici, Ciel, Cierra, Cindy, Claire, Clara, Clarabelle, Clare, Clarice, Claris, Clarissa, Clarisse, Clarity, Clary, Claudette, Claudia, Claudine, Clea, Clementine, Cleo, Cleopatra, Clodagh, Clotilde, Clover, Coco, Colette, Colleen, Connie, Constance, Cora, Coral, Coralie, Coraline, Cordelia, Cori, Corina, Corinne, Cornelia, Corra, Cosette, Courtney, Cressida, Cristal, Cristina, Crystal, Cynthia. Dagmar, Dahlia, Daisy, Dakota, Dana, Danette, Dani, Danica, Daniela, Daniella, Danielle, Danika, Daphne, Dara, Darby, Darcey, Darcie, Darcy, Daria, Darla, Darlene, Dasia, Davida, Davina, Dawn, Dayna, Daysha, Deana, Deandra, Deann, Deanna, Deanne, Deb, Debbie, Debby, Debora, Deborah, Debra, Dee, Deedee, Deena, Deidre, Deirdre, Deja, Delaney, Delanie, Delany, Delia, Delilah, Della, Delores, Delphine, Demetria, Demi, Dena, Denise, Denny, Desiree, Destinee, Destiny, Diamond, Diana, Diane, Dianna, Dianne, Dido, Dina, Dionne, Dior, Dixie, Dolly, Dolores, Dominique, Donna, Dora, Doreen, Doris, Dorothy, Dot, Drew, Dulce. Eabha, Ebony, Echo, Eden, Edie, Edith, Edna, Edwina, Effie, Eileen, Eilidh, Eimear, Elaina, Elaine, Elana, Eleanor, Electra, Elektra, Elena, Eliana, Elin, Elina, Elinor, Elisa, Elisabeth, Elise, Eliza, Elizabeth, Ella, Elle, Ellen, Ellery, Ellie, Ellis, Elly, Elodie, Eloise, Elora, Elsa, Elsie, Elspeth, Elva, Elvira, Elysia, Elyza, Emanuela, Ember, Emelda, Emely, Emer, Emerald, Emerson, Emilee, Emilia, Emilie, Emily, Emma, Emmalee, Emmaline, Emmalyn, Emmanuelle, Emmeline, Emmie, Emmy, Enya, Erica, Erika, Erin, Eris, Eryn, Esmay, Esme, Esmeralda, Esperanza, Estee, Estelle, Ester, Esther, Estrella, Ethel, Eugenie, Eunice, Eva, Evangelina, Evangeline, Eve, Evelin, Evelyn, Everly, Evie, Evita. Fabrizia, Faith, Fallon, Fanny, Farah, Farrah, Fatima, Fawn, Fay, Faye, Felicia, Felicity, Fern, Fernanda, Ffion, Fifi, Fiona, Fleur, Flick, Flo, Flora, Florence, Fran, Frances, Francesca, Francine, Frankie, Freda, Freya, Frida. Gabby, Gabriela, Gabriella, Gabrielle, Gail, Gayle, Gaynor, Geena, Gemma, Gena, Genesis, Genevieve, Georgette, Georgia, Georgie, Georgina, Geraldine, Gert, Gertrude, Gia, Gianna, Gigi, Gillian, Gina, Ginger, Ginny, Giovanna, Gisela, Giselle, Gisselle, Gladys, Glenda, Glenys, Gloria, Golda, Grace, Gracelyn, Gracie, Grainne, Greta, Gretchen, Griselda, Guadalupe, Guinevere, Gwen, Gwendolyn, Gwyneth. Habiba, Hadley, Hailee,

Hailey, Haleigh, Haley, Halle, Hallie, Hanna, Hannah, Harley, Harmony, Harper, Harriet, Hattie, Haven, Hayden, Haylee, Hayley, Hazel, Hazeline, Heather, Heaven, Heidi, Helen, Helena, Helene, Helga, Helina, Henrietta, Hepsiba, Hera, Hermione, Hester, Hetty, Hilary, Hilda, Hillary, Hollie, Holly, Honesty, Honey, Honor, Honour, Hope, Hyacinth. Ianthe, Ida, Ila, Ilene, Iliana, Ilona, Ilse, Imani, Imelda, Imogen, India, Indie, Indigo, Indira, Ines, Ingrid, Iona, Ira, Irene, Irina, Iris, Irma, Isa, Isabel, Isabell, Isabella, Isabelle, Isadora, Isha, Isis, Isla, Isobel, Isolde, Itzel, Ivana, Ivy, Iyanna, Izabella, Izidora, Izzie, Izzy. Jacinda, Jacinta, Jackie, Jacqueline, Jacquelyn, Jada, Jade, Jaden, Jadyn, Jaelynn, Jaida, Jaime, Jamie, Jamiya, Jan, Jana, Jancis, Jane, Janelle, Janessa, Janet, Janette, Jania, Janice, Janie, Janine, Janis, Janiya, January, Jaqueline, Jasmin, Jasmine, Jaya, Jayda, Jayden, Jayla, Jaylene, Jaylinn, Jaylynn, Jayne, Jazlyn, Jazmin, Jazmine, Jean, Jeanette, Jeanine, Jeanne, Jeannette, Jeannie, Jeannine, Jemima, Jemma, Jen, Jena, Jenelle, Jenessa, Jenna, Jennette, Jenni, Jennie, Jennifer, Jenny, Jensen, Jeri, Jerri, Jess, Jessa, Jessica, Jessie, Jet, Jewel, Jill, Jillian, Jo, Joan, Joann, Joanna, Joanne, Jocelyn, Jodi, Jodie, Jody, Joelle, Johanna, Joleen, Jolene, Jolie, Joni, Jordan, Jordana, Jordyn, Jorja, Joselyn, Josephine, Josie, Joy, Joyce, Juanita, Jude, Judith, Judy, Jules, Julia, Juliana, Julianna, Julianne, Julie, Julienne, Juliet, Juliette, Julissa, July, June, Juniper, Juno, Justice, Justina, Justine. Kacey, Kadence, Kaidence, Kailey, Kailyn, Kaitlin, Kaitlyn, Kaitlynn, Kalea, Kaleigh, Kali, Kalia, Kamala, Kamryn, Kara, Karen, Kari, Karin, Karina, Karissa, Karla, Karlee, Karly, Karolina, Karyn, Kasey, Kassandra, Kassidy, Kassie, Kat, Katara, Katarina, Kate, Katelyn, Katelynn, Katerina, Katharine, Katherine, Kathleen, Kathryn, Kathy, Katia, Katie, Katlyn, Katniss, Katrina, Katy, Katya, Kay, Kaya, Kaye, Kayla, Kaylee, Kayleigh, Kayley, Kaylie, Kaylin, Keara, Keeley, Keely, Keira, Keisha, Kelis, Kelley, Kelli, Kellie, Kelly, Kelsey, Kelsie, Kendall, Kendra, Kenna, Kennedy, Kenzie, Kera, Keri, Kerian, Kerri, Kerry, Kia, Kiana, Kiara, Kiera, Kierra, Kiersten, Kiki, Kiley, Kim, Kimberlee, Kimberley, Kimberly, Kimbriella, Kimmy, Kinley, Kinsey, Kinsley, Kira, Kirsten, Kirstin, Kirsty, Kitty, Kizzy, Kloe, Kora, Kori, Kourtney, Kris, Krista, Kristen, Kristi, Kristie, Kristin, Kristina, Kristine, Kristy, Krystal, Kyla, Kylee, Kyleigh, Kylie, Kyra. Lacey, Lacie, Lacy, Ladonna, Laila, Lainey, Lakyn, Lala, Lana, Laney, Lara, Larissa, Latoya, Laura, Laurel, Lauren, Laurie, Lauryn, Lavana, Lavender, Lavinia, Layla, Lea, Leah, Leandra, Leann, Leanna, Leanne, Lee, Leela, Leena, Leia, Leigh, Leila, Leilani, Lela, Lena, Lenore, Leona, Leonie, Leora, Lesley, Leslie, Lesly, Leticia, Lettie, Lexi, Lexia, Lexie, Lexis, Lia, Liana, Lianne, Libbie, Libby, Liberty, Lidia, Liesl, Lila, Lilac, Lilah, Lili, Lilian, Liliana, Lilita, Lilith, Lillia, Lillian, Lillie, Lilly, Lily, Lina, Linda, Lindsay, Lindsey, Lindy, Lisa, Lisette, Liv, Livia, Livvy, Liz, Liza, Lizbeth, Lizette, Lizzie, Lizzy,

Logan, Lois, Lola, Lolita, London, Lora, Loran, Lorelei, Loren, Lorena, Loretta, Lori, Lorie, Lorna, Lorraine, Lorri, Lorrie, Lottie, Lotus, Lou, Louisa, Louise, Luann, Lucia, Luciana, Lucie, Lucille, Lucinda, Lucky, Lucy, Luisa, Lulu, Luna, Lupita, Luz, Lydia, Lyla, Lynda, Lyndsey, Lynette, Lynn, Lynne, Lynnette, Lynsey, Lyra, Lyric. Mabel, Macey, Macie, Mackenzie, Macy, Madalyn, Maddie, Maddison, Maddy, Madeleine, Madeline, Madelyn, Madison, Madisyn, Madonna, Madyson, Mae, Maeve, Magda, Magdalena, Magdalene, Maggie, Maia, Maire, Mairead, Maisie, Maisy, Maja, Makayla, Makenna, Makenzie, Malia, Malina, Malinda, Mallory, Malory, Mandy, Manuela, Mara, Marcela, Marcella, Marci, Marcia, Marcie, Marcy, Margaret, Margarita, Margaux, Marge, Margie, Margo, Margot, Margret, Maria, Mariah, Mariam, Marian, Mariana, Marianna, Marianne, Maribel, Marie, Mariela, Mariella, Marilyn, Marina, Marion, Marisa, Marisol, Marissa, Maritza, Marjorie, Marla, Marlee, Marlena, Marlene, Marley, Marnie, Marsha, Martha, Martina, Mary, Maryam, Maryann, Marybeth, Masie, Matilda, Maude, Maura, Maureen, Mavis, Maxine, May, Maya, Mazie, Mckayla, Mckenna, Mckenzie, Mea, Meadow, Meagan, Meera, Meg, Megan, Meghan, Mei, Mel, Melanie, Melina, Melinda, Melissa, Melody, Mercedes, Mercy, Meredith, Merida, Meryl, Mia, Michaela, Michele, Michelle, Mika, Mikaela, Mikayla, Mikhaela, Mila, Mildred, Milena, Miley, Millicent, Millie, Milly, Mimi, Mina, Mindy, Minerva, Minnie, Mira, Mirabel, Mirabelle, Miracle, Miranda, Miriam, Missie, Misty, Mitzi, Moira, Mollie, Molly, Mona, Monica, Monika, Monique, Montana, Morgan, Morgana, Moya, Muriel, Mya, Myfanwy, Myla, Myra, Myrna, Myrtle. Nadene, Nadia, Nadine, Naja, Nala, Nana, Nancy, Nanette, Naomi, Natalia, Natalie, Natasha, Naya, Nayeli, Nell, Nellie, Nelly, Nena, Nerissa, Nessa, Nevaeh, Neve, Nia, Niamh, Nichola, Nichole, Nicki, Nicky, Nicola, Nicole, Nicolette, Nieve, Niki, Nikita, Nikki, Nila, Nina, Nishka, Noelle, Noemi, Nola, Nora, Norah, Noreen, Norma, Nova, Nyla. Oasis, Ocean, Octavia, Odalis, Odele, Odelia, Odette, Olga, Olive, Olivia, Oona, Oonagh, Opal, Ophelia, Oriana, Orianna, Orla, Orlaith. Page, Paige, Paisley, Paloma, Pam, Pamela, Pandora, Pansy, Paola, Paris, Parker, Patience, Patrice, Patricia, Patsy, Patti, Patty, Paula, Paulette, Paulina, Pauline, Payton, Peace, Pearl, Peggy, Penelope, Penny, Perla, Perrie, Persephone, Petra, Petunia, Peyton, Phillipa, Philomena, Phoebe, Phoenix, Phyllis, Piper, Pippa, Pixie, Polly, Poppy, Portia, Precious, Presley, Preslie, Primrose, Princess, Priscilla, Priya, Promise, Prudence, Prue. Queenie, Quiana, Quinn. Rabia, Rachael, Rachel, Rachelle, Rae, Raegan, Raelyn, Raina, Raine, Ramona, Ramsha, Randi, Rani, Rania, Raquel, Raven, Raya, Rayna, Rayne, Reagan, Reanna, Reanne, Rebecca, Rebekah, Reed, Reese, Regan, Regina, Reilly, Reina, Remi, Rena, Renata, Rene, Renee, Renesmee, Reyna, Rhea, Rhian, Rhianna, Rhiannon, Rhoda, Rhona, Rhonda, Ria, Rianna, Ricki, Rihanna, Rikki,

Riley, Rita, River, Riya, Roanne, Roberta, Robin, Robyn, Rochelle, Rocio, Roisin, Rolanda, Ronda, Roni, Rosa, Rosalie, Rosalina, Rosalind, Rosalinda, Rosalynn, Rosanna, Rose, Roseanne, Rosella, Rosemarie, Rosemary, Rosetta, Rosie, Rosy, Rowan, Rowena, Roxana, Roxanne, Roxie, Roxy, Rozlynn, Ruby, Rue, Ruth, Ruthie, Rydel, Rylee, Ryleigh, Rylie. Sabina, Sabine, Sable, Sabrina, Sade, Sadhbh, Sadie, Saffron, Safire, Safiya, Sage, Sahara, Saige, Saira, Sally, Salma, Salome, Sam, Samantha, Samara, Samia, Samira, Sammie, Sammy, Sandra, Sandy, Saoirse, Sapphire, Sara, Sarah, Sarina, Sariya, Sascha, Sasha, Saskia, Savanna, Savannah, Scarlet, Scarlett, Sebastianne, Selah, Selena, Selene, Selina, Selma, Senuri, September, Seren, Serena, Serenity, Shakira, Shana, Shania, Shannon, Shari, Sharon, Shary, Shauna, Shawn, Shawna, Shawnette, Shayla, Shayna, Shea, Sheena, Sheila, Shelby, Shelia, Shelley, Shelly, Sheri, Sheridan, Sherri, Sherrie, Sherry, Sheryl, Shirley, Shivani, Shona, Shreya, Shyla, Sian, Sidney, Sienna, Sierra, Sigourney, Silvia, Simone, Simran, Sinead, Siobhan, Sky, Skye, Skylar, Skyler, Sloane, Snow, Sofia, Sofie, Sondra, Sonia, Sonja, Sonya, Sophia, Sophie, Sophy, Spring, Stacey, Staci, Stacie, Stacy, Star, Starla, Stefanie, Stella, Steph, Stephanie, Sue, Suki, Summer, Susan, Susanna, Susannah, Susanne, Susie, Sutton, Suzanna, Suzanne, Suzette, Suzie, Suzy, Sybil, Sydney, Sylvia, Sylvie. Tabatha, Tabitha, Tahlia, Tala, Talia, Talitha, Taliyah, Tallulah, Tamara, Tamera, Tami, Tamia, Tamika, Tammi, Tammie, Tammy, Tamra, Tamsin, Tania, Tanisha, Tanya, Tara, Taryn, Tasha, Tasmin, Tatiana, Tatum, Tawana, Taya, Tayla, Taylah, Tayler, Taylor, Teagan, Teegan, Tegan, Teigan, Tenille, Teresa, Teri, Terri, Terrie, Terry, Tess, Tessa, Thalia, Thea, Thelma, Theodora, Theresa, Therese, Thomasina, Tia, Tiana, Tiegan, Tiffany, Tilly, Tina, Tisha, Toni, Tonia, Tonya, Tori, Tracey, Traci, Tracie, Tracy, Tricia, Trina, Trinity, Trish, Trisha, Trista, Trixie, Trixy, Trudy, Tula, Tulip, Tyra. Ulrica, Uma, Una, Ursula. Valarie, Valentina, Valeria, Valerie, Vanessa, Veda, Velma, Venetia, Venus, Vera, Verity, Veronica, Vicki, Vickie, Vicky, Victoria, Vienna, Viola, Violet, Violetta, Virginia, Vivian, Viviana, Vivien, Vivienne. Wallis, Wanda, Waverley, Wendi, Wendy, Whitney, Wilhelmina, Willa, Willow, Wilma, Winnie, Winnifred, Winona, Winter. Xandra, Xanthe, Xaviera, Xena, Xia, Ximena, Xochil, Xochitl. Yasmin, Yasmine, Yazmin, Yelena, Yesenia, Yolanda, Ysabel, Yulissa, Yvaine, Yvette, Yvonne. Zada, Zaheera, Zahra, Zaira, Zakia, Zali, Zara, Zaria, Zaya, Zayla, Zelda, Zelida, Zelina, Zena, Zendaya, Zia, Zina, Ziva, Zoe, Zoey, Zola, Zora, Zoya, Zula, Zuri, Zyana.

## (C): A Brief Account of the Sandwich (MA) Courthouse (from *A Metamodernist's Guide to Cape Cod*)

As anyone who's been there knows, Sandwich is the oldest town on Cape Cod. It earned that title when it incorporated in 1637, though when it disincorporated in 1639 it lost the title to neighboring Barnstable, which was the oldest town on Cape Cod between its incorporation in 1638 and Sandwich's reincorporation in 1639. Despite the reemergence of Sandwich, Eastham was the oldest town on Cape Cod from 1640 to 1642, as the elders of Barnstable had decreed in 1639 that the borders of Cape Cod extended only so far as Creek's Crick, which was dug out by Mortimer Creek in 1643 and finally declared a creek in 1944. In 1645, Mashpee briefly usurped the title of oldest town on Cape Cod from the resurgent Sandwich when it was revealed that its Town Hall had been built in 1633, though it lost the title in 1637 when it was subsequently discovered that the Town Hall in Mashpee had been founded as the Mashpee Annex for Unincorporated Persons. When it was renamed the Mashpee Town Hall in 1646, Mashpee was briefly the oldest town on Cape Cod, Sandwich having been tragically destroyed by fire in 1645. "Sandwich," rebuilt in 1651, was named the oldest town on Cape Cod for the first time in 1652, when it was revealed that it had been rebuilt atop the ruins of Winchendon, indisputably the oldest settlement on Cape Code but abandoned during an attack by the Nauset tribe in 1631. The Town of Winchendon, removed to an off-Cape location and eventually incorporated in 1874, was therefore the oldest town on Cape Cod between 1654 and 1656, during which time the rebuilt Sandwich was being moved back to its original location a half-mile north, a transport that inadvertently resulted in the razing of the Village of Canterbury, a settlement that had incorporated in 1636 with just three families and two buildings, one a courthouse and one an outhouse servicing the courthouse and its immediate environs. The Truro Courthouse, used for theater productions only, was at the time of the off-Cape Winchendon's incorporation the oldest structure on the Cape, having been built with wood from the fence of the Canterbury outhouse in 1873, after the Sandwich courthouse that replaced the Canterbury outhouse (partially built with Canterbury wood) was deeded to the British town of Sandwich (founded in 1028) in 1690, in partial recompense for the use of that town's name by "Sandwich" beginning in 1637. By 1691, Brewster shared the title of oldest town on Cape Cod with Sandwich, a gesture of friendship between the city Fathers of each, Brewster's first twenty Fathers having previously been among the first ten of Sandwich. Brewster maintained its claim to the title of "oldest tune on Cape Cod" after the souring of relations with England's Sandwich in 1692, whereupon it deeded its claim as oldest town on Cape Cod to Truro, which held the title jointly with the British Sandwich (albeit contested on the latter side) until 1701, when Truro was incorporated into Wellfleet. (That incorporation was undone in 1877 as part of celebrations commemorating the re-commemoration of the Truro Outhouse.) Between 1701 and 1710, the Commonwealth of Massachusetts, unnerved by recent Native American incursions, disbanded all incorporated towns on Cape Code via receivership, the end of which receivership led to all Cape towns then extant (other than Sandwich) claiming the title of oldest town on Cape Cod in 1711. In 1731, Sandwich purchased the oldest-town claims of Provincetown, Cotuit, Chatham, and Falmouth, thereby securing eleven votes for Sandwich as oldest town on Cape Cod during the era of the Cape Cod Regional Council, a body which met once every three years between 1731 and 1733. In 1935, the Council's headquarters were forcefully moved off-Cape by a spring tornado, ending forthwith (per by-laws) the Council's sixteen-mile jurisdiction over the Lower Cape. In response, Harwichport, a village in the Lower Cape's Town of Harwich—the first municipal sub-unit designated a "village" in Cape history—decreed itself Oldest Village on the Cape in 1934. There was no dissent at the time, though since then the designation has been met with unanimous approval. Harwichport's 1934 power-grab was followed hard upon by the Capetown development within the Town of Harwich claiming the designation of oldest Cape-town in the U.S. in 1936. That designation was sold back to the British Sandwich in 1947 for a symbolic $16.37, a gesture of goodwill following the slaughter of 28 U.S. infantrymen from Sandwich at Normandy. A miniature of Provincetown's famous Normandy War Memorial statue can be purchased at <u>this</u> link.

## (D): Sonnet 2013

http://www.bbc.co.uk/news/world-africa-21042659
http://www.telegraph.co.uk/health/healthnews/9883441/
Scientists-create-artificial-ear-using-3D-printing-and-living-
cell-gels.html
http://www.bbc.co.uk/news/world-europe-21777494
http://edition.cnn.com/2013/04/15/us/boston-marathon-
explosions/

http://www.nature.com/news/human-stem-cells-created-by-
cloning-1.12983
http://www.theguardian.com/world/2013/jun/23/edward-
snowden-nsa-files-timeline?INTCMP=SRCH
http://edition.cnn.com/2013/07/03/world/meast/egypt-
protests/index.html?hpt=hp_t1
http://www.cbsnews.com/news/human-rights-watch-says-
evidence-strongly-suggests-assad-used-chemical-weapons/

http://www.bbc.co.uk/news/world-africa-24189116
http://www.mediaite.com/tv/a-brief-history-of-the-2013-
government-shutdown/
http://www.bbc.co.uk/news/world-asia-24887337
http://www.bbc.co.uk/news/science-environment-25356603

http://www.youtube.com/watch?v=JoyUUokcX5g
http://www.youtube.com/watch?v=_dJCLaoBZvM

**"White Privilege"** comprises 650 true statements about the author, written by the author.

**"Strangers"** comprises 325 statements made about the author between 2008 and 2015. All of these statements were made by individuals the author had not met at the time the statement was made. In a handful of cases, a single speaker was responsible for several successive statements.

**Section II of *DATA*** comprises fifteen lyric poems composed using two- to four-word phrases taken from a series of multi-hour lectures on the avant-garde delivered by University of Wisconsin-Madison Professor Cyrena Pondrom in 2012; a maximum of ten word-substitutions were permitted per poem, though most poems use six or fewer. Two other poems—**"Defeat at Krasny Bor, the Green Boxes, and the New Order of March"** and **"As Explanation"**—use (respectively) Tristan Tzara's 1918 "Dada Manifesto" and Gertrude Stein's 1925 "Composition As Explanation" as their source texts. **"The Revolution for Some"** is a "reflexive remix" (a remix of a poem's first draft). **"Pater Familias"** is an unaltered original text.

The first section of **"The Metamodernist Manifesto"** is a collage of 125 independent clauses or otherwise discrete declarations verbalized by the author on November 10, 2013. None of the clauses contiguous here were contiguous in their original context. For the purposes of this poem, each clause has been made to end in either a period or a colon. The second section of the poem comprises 20 clicks of the "Generate Status" button on the "What Would I Say?" website (http://what-would-i-say.com/). "What Would I Say?" approximates a Facebook user's (in this case, the author's) "average" Facebook status using text and compositional proclivities from prior status updates published by the user. The text produced by the website has been subjectively "normalized" by the author with regard to grammar, syntax, punctuation, and typography. The semantic content of these "average" Facebook statuses has not been changed. The third section of the poem is a collage of results returned from the author's responses to eight "What Your Taste Says About You on a Date" quizzes. These quizzes asked readers to name their favorite bands, TV shows, drinks, ice cream, books, footwear, sex positions, and sports teams.

The section of **"Oh People"** that appears here comprises 120 sentences from the status updates of the first one hundred Facebook accounts appearing in the author's "Close Friends" news feed on September 19-20, 2013. These accounts belong to the following individuals and organizations: Eduardo Corral, Lemon Hound, Johannes Göransson, Sampson Starkweather, John Gallaher, Spencer Short, Metta Sama, David Shapiro, Amy King, Robert Lee Brewer, David Biespiel, Ron Silliman, Matthew Nienow, Ada Limon, Allison Joseph, Julie Larson-Guenette, Camille Dungy, Sandra Simonds, Alan Felsenthal, Adam Fell, Corey Zeller, Kyle McCord, Brandon Amico, Gabrielle Calvocoressi, Craig Teicher, Anselm Berrigan, Shane McCrae, Matthew Burnside, Emily Kendal Frey, Gabriel Gudding, Bradley Harrison Smith, Sandra Beasley, Stephen Burt, William Stobb, Don Share, Daisy Fried, Ryan Collins, Joyelle McSweeney, C. Dale Young, Laura Eve Engel, Lina Ramona Vitkauskas, Jazzy Danziger Loyal, Paula Neuhaus, Michael Kasden, Stanley Todd-Hume Swift, Kirsten Hotelling Zona, Sterling Holywhitemountain, Charles Bernstein, Brooklyn Copeland Seall, Matthew Guenette, Larry Sawyer, Josh Fomon, Rusty Morrison, Oliver Bendorf, Janet Holmes, YesYes Books, Ben Mazer, Chloe Zwiacher, Zachary Schomburg, Stacey Lynn Brown, Matthias Svalina, Arielle Bernstein, Ben Fama, Adam Fitzgerald, Alfred Corn, Josh Kalscheur, Charles Jensen, Robert Archambeau, Nate Brown, Tom Kealey, Michael Mlekoday, Jamie Iredell, Timothy Yu, Emileigh Barnes Williams, Tim Earley, Erica Bernheim, Rachel Abramowitz, Mark Doty, Magdelena Zurawski, Trey Gulledge, Nick Sturm, Sean Bishop, Louis Armand, David Blumenshine, Kenzie Allen, Nayelly Barrios, Jesse Lee Kercheval, T.R. Hummer, Cate Marvin, Nick Lantz, Ash Bowen, Rauan Klassnik, Francesco Levato, Autumn Elizabeth, Oliver de la Paz, Lily Duffy, Dawn Lonsinger, Traci Brimhall, Ashley Anna McHugh, and Willow Springs.

**"My Screen"** is a collage of all words appearing in the author's main browser window at 5PM on November 25th, 2013.

**"Four-Tab Weave"** is an interweaving of texts appearing in four tabs of the author's web browser on April 3rd, 2015: a poem by Robert Frost; a spam ad (arrived at pursuant to a clandestine re-direct from *The Sycamore Review* website); the lyrics to a song from *The Last Unicorn*, performed by the band America; and a draft of a note the author wrote to himself.

**"Calvin & Hobbes & Susie"** is a collage of a hundred statements made by the author's girlfriend and closest male friend during the month of October in 2013. Permission from both parties was obtained beforehand, though neither knew when their words would be recorded or which of their words would be used. The sequencing of statements was only determined by the author once all hundred statements had been collected. Only full sentences or phrases of ten or more words were used for this collage. In five instances, conjunctions were added to a sentence or phrase.

**"Amoral"** is at least three consecutive words from every page of a trade paperback of *The Secret Six* (DC Comics), arranged sequentially in the order these phrases appeared in the comic.

**"All You Ploughboys (*)"** is an erasure of workshop comments the author received on the poem "All You Ploughboys," whose original text appeared in the collection *Thievery* (University of Akron Press, 2013). Eight pages of workshop comments from a University of Wisconsin-Madison course were used for the creation of this poem; each stanza in the poem is attributable to a discrete comment sheet, though most comment sheets contributed more than one stanza.

The section of **"The Motto of the Internet"** that appears here juxtaposes a hundred phrases taken from the author's Twitter feed on October 21-22, 2013. These phrases all met the following requirements: were five words or more; did not comprise the totality of a tweet; and were written by the first hundred individuals (not institutions) with original or shared (not merely "retweeted") content appearing in the author's Twitter feed. The hundred individuals whose public statements appear in "The Motto of the Internet" are the following discrete Twitter users: Marina Weiss, Julia Fiero, Mikey Swanberg, Alex Lemon, Richard Krawiec, D.A. Powell, Benjamin Hale, Rachel Burns, Dobby Gibson, Patricia Caspers, Nate Knapp, Daniel Casey, Jon Winokur, Porochista Khakpour, Sam Witt, Kara Monterey, Chris Fischbach, Danielle Burhop, Samuel Amadon, Michaela Watkins, Tyler Mills, Matthew Zoller Seitz, Michael Strahan, Carolyn Kellogg, Danielle Douglas, Yiyun Li, Alexander Chee, Kris Bigalk, Evan Munday, Seth Abramson, Elizabeth McCracken, Leah Umansky, Jillian York, Shelly Farmer, Maureen Johnson, Ben Greenman, Justin Marks, Daniel Nester, Ben Steil, Eduardo C. Corral, Lemon Hound, Kima Jones, Rob Spillman, Patrick Healy, Dawn Martin Lundy, Cody Klippenstein, Collin Kelley, Portia Elan, Joan Walsh, Peter Hoffman, Jonathan Crowl, Hannah Stephenson, Hannah Faye, Joanna Coles, James Patterson, Joe Briggs; Kenzo Shibata, Timothy Michael Law, Joshua Corey, Carrie Murphy, Ted Cruz, Don Lewis, Jeffrey Simpson, Sampson Starkweather, Kimberly Southwick, Margo Rabb, Stephen Colbert, Sally Jenkins, Elizabeth Stelling, Chris Herring, Bill Ryan, Tom Beer, Christina

McTighe, Kylan Rice, Adam Roberts, Gina Myers, Andres Rojas, Matt Ford, Erica Wright, Brett LoGiurato, Nic Bishop, Matt Drudge, David Marshall, Lisa Rosman, Brandon Amico, Hannah Goldfield, Mary Beth Williams, Meg Pokrass, Jessie Carty, Angie LeMar, David Biespiel, Bill Herbert, Ruth Konigsberg, Maureen Doallas, Deborah Netburn, George Szirtes, Marco Fernando Navarro, James Everington, Miriam Rule, Matt Bell, Lisa Kerr, and Christopher Hayes.

**"James Franco By James Franco By Seth Abramson"** is a remix of James Franco's chapbook *Strongest of the Litter* (Hollyridge Press, 2012). Each line of Section I is taken (in whole) from one of the following four poems in *Strongest of the Litter*: "Florida Sex Scene," "Seventh Grade," "Elizabeth Taylor," or "Montgomery Clift"; each line of Section II is taken from "Art School," "Historical," "Whales," or "Gay New York"; each line of Section III is taken from "Fifth Grade," "Theater," "Double," or "Montgomery Clift"; each line of Section IV is taken from "Fake," "My Name Is Paterson," "Paterson History," or "Marlon Brando"; each line of Section V is taken from "Paterson Love," "De Niro," or "Blue Being"; and each line of Section VI is taken from "Animals," "Death," "Nocturnal," "Telephone," or the chapbook's Table of Contents.

**"Bear, Son"** is a remix of Matthew Zapruder's poem "Sun Bear." Typeface, conjunctions, and punctuation have been added or amended. In several instances, homonyms were used. (The full text of Zapruder's poem can be found at http://www.blackbird.vcu.edu/v11n2/poetry/zapruder_m/bear_page.shtml.)

**"Stalker #102"** remixes the lines of the Beach Boys' 1964 pop ballad "Girl Don't Tell Me."

**"E-Death #4"** is a stanza-by-stanza remix of the song "Marching Bands of Manhattan," the opening track on Death Cab for Cutie's 2005 album *Plans*. (The song's lyrics: http://songmeanings.com/songs/view/3530822107858551145/.)

**"Friday"** is a stanza-by-stanza remix of the pop song "Friday" by Rebecca Black. The words of each stanza in the song's lyric sheet were rearranged in-stanza; the stanzas were then ordered sequentially. Duplicate stanzas (i.e., repeated bridges or choruses) were not used for this remix.

**"Thirteen Ways of Looking at a Blackbird"** is a mash-up of the song "Blackbird" (written by Paul McCartney) and Wallace Stevens' poem "Thirteen Ways of Looking at a Blackbird." (To read the lyrics of the song "Blackbird", see http://www.azlyrics.com/lyrics/paulmccartney/blackbird.html; Stevens' poem: http://www.writing.upenn.edu/~afilreis/88/stevens-13ways.html.) The order of lines in the original works has been amended, and punctuation, typeface, and enjambment have been altered. Otherwise, the individual lines remain intact.

**"Battle of the Bands"** is composed entirely of band names (along with several conjunctions).

The first twenty-two lines of **"The Damn Day"** appeared in the author's 2011 poetry collection, *Northerners* (New Issues/Western Michigan University Press). The final lines are the script of a 2013 Kia television commercial.

**"Homewrecker"** reprints three consecutive Google Maps query results. "X" indicates the  route selected by the querying party ("the user"). Arrows indicate the actual path taken.

**"The Road Not Taken By Robert Frost"** adds six words to the original text of Robert Frost's "The Road Not Taken"—three in the title and three in the poem.

**"New York Times 5 Notable Poetry Books of 2013"** (Appendix A) is a complete list of the poetry books the *New York Times* listed in its rundown of 2013's "100 best books."

**"A Brief Account of the Sandwich (MA) Courthouse"** (Appendix C) owes a debt to the performance art of Reggie Watts, which plays with both factuality and cogency.

The first twelve lines of **"Sonnet 2013"** (Appendix D) comprise links to one of the most significant news stories of each of the twelve months of 2013. The final couplet comprises two YouTube videos: one of a sunrise on an "unremarkable" day, and one of a sunset on a similarly unremarkable day.

*Acknowledgments*

My sincere thanks to the editors of *Barn Owl Review* ("Love Story"); *Brooklyn Rail* ("Coming About," "Contradictory Elements in the Personal History of Djuna Barnes," "Europa," and "On the Phalanx in History"); *Diode* ("Lecture"); *From the Fishouse* ("Amoral," "The Damn Day," and "White Privilege"); *Ink Node* ("All You Ploughboys*", "An Alphabetical Index of Significant Manic Pixie Dream Girls," "Calvin & Hobbes & Susie," "James Franco By James Franco By Seth Abramson," "Mid-America," "from 'Oh People'", and "*New York Times* 5 Notable Books of 2013"); *The Good Men Project* ("Right Bank"); *Similar Peaks* ("Descending into the Bloody Stag to Meet the Boys," "Girl in a Girl in a Chinese Room," and "Maybe I Would Love It in the West"); and *VLAK* ("A Brief Account of the Sandwich [MA] Courthouse," "Animalia," "E-Death #4," "Friday," "from 'The Motto of the Internet'", "Homewrecker," "The Metamodernist Manifesto," "My Screen," "The Road Not Taken By Robert Frost," "Seth Abramson!", and "Sonnet 7c"). Special thanks to Professor Emeritus Cyrena Pondrom of the University of Wisconsin-Madison, whose erudite lectures inspired much thought and reflection in addition to the poetry seen here.

Without the love, advice, and encouragement of my wife, Danielle Burhop, neither this book nor anything resembling a happy life would be possible for me.

Additional thanks to all those whose inspiration, affection, and support helped make this book a reality. An admittedly incomplete list of those whose influence on this book was significant would include Claudia Abramson, Robert Abramson, David Avital, Amy Quan Barry, Sean Bishop, Paul Borchardt, Bo Burnham, Brian Christian, Kirsten Clodfelter, Jesse Damiani, Alexandra Dumitrescu, Donald Dunbar, Eden Dunckel, Eric Dunckel, Eva Dunckel, James Franco, Josh Freeman, Geoffrey Gatza, Wade Geary, Donald Glover, Melvin Gordon III, Dan Harmon, Matthew Herman, Sterling Holywhitemountain, Amaud Jamaul Johnson, Josh Kalscheur, Andrew Kay, Douglas Kearney, Christopher Kempf, Jesse Lee Kercheval, Ron Kuka, Jane Lewty, Vicente López, Judy Mitchell, Seamus Moran, Haruki Murakami, Carrie Seitzinger, Michael Shea, Sturgill Simpson, Jaden Smith, Neal Stephenson, William Stobb, Cole Swensen, Suzanna Tamminen, Hans Teeuwen, Corey Van Landingham, David Foster Wallace, Ron Wallace, Reggie Watts, Max Winter, Steven Wright, Mas'ud Zavarzadeh, Josh Zifcak, Kevin Zifcak, Lily Zifcak, Sarah Zifcak, Stephen Zrike, and the students from my Fall 2014 "Metamodernism in Popular Culture" and Spring 2015 "Intermediate Creative Writing" courses at University of Wisconsin.

Finally, sincere thanks to all those individuals mentioned on pp. 148-150, whose public statements on social media have been so briefly excerpted here that none can be readily traced to their authors, but whose wit, candor, and verbal acuity has inspired me not only through the poems of this collection but also in my daily writing, reading, and imagining.

**Seth Abramson** is the Series Editor for *Best American Experimental Writing* and an assistant professor of English at University of New Hampshire. Author of six books, he writes on metamodernism for *The Huffington Post* and *Indiewire*. In 2015 he published a prequel to *DATA*, *Metamericana*, with BlazeVOX Books.

Made in the USA
Monee, IL
07 July 2026